THE SENIOR INTERNATIONAL OFFICER AS CHANGE AGENT

THE SENIOR INTERNATIONAL OFFICER AS CHANGE AGENT

John D. Heyl and Fiona J. H. Hunter

Second Edition

Distributed by

AIEA
Leaders in International Higher Education

Sty/us

STERLING, VIRGINIA

COPYRIGHT © 2019 BY AIEA

Distributed by Stylus Publishing, LLC.
22883 Quicksilver Drive
Sterling, Virginia 20166-2019

Library of Congress Cataloging-in-Publication Data
CIP data for this title has been applied for.

13-digit ISBN: 978-1-62036-958-6 (cloth)
13-digit ISBN: 978-1-62036-959-3 (paperback)
13-digit ISBN: 978-1-62036-960-9 (library networkable e-edition)
13-digit ISBN: 978-1-62036-961-6 (consumer e-edition)

Printed in the United States of America

All first editions printed on acid-free paper
that meets the American National Standards Institute
Z39-48 Standard.

Bulk Purchases
Quantity discounts are available for use in workshops and for staff development.
Call 1-800-232-0223

Second Edition, 2019

CONTENTS

ACKNOWLEDGMENTS

The authors wish to thank Darla K. Deardorff, Association of International Education Administrators (AIEA) executive director, and Amir Reza, AIEA editorial committee chair, for their encouragement and assistance in rethinking the earlier edition of *The Senior International Officer (SIO) as Change Agent* (AIEA, 2007). We also appreciate the guidance provided by McKenzie Baker and her Stylus colleagues through the final editing process. Finally, we offer special thanks to those senior international officers who have shared reflections on their careers directly with us and in their published writing.

INTRODUCTION

*Good leaders are by definition change agents, taking their
institutions to greater heights of excellence and service.*

—Madeleine F. Green and Christa L. Olson (2003)

*To accomplish the task of internationalization . . . requires knowledge
about change, for internationalization is about change and the future.*

—Josef Mestenhauser and Brenda Ellingboe (2005)

*We should be "the broker": always looking to build internal
linkages. We should multi-task and be comfortable wearing more
than one hat. And lastly, we should never stop learning.*

—Hans-Georg van Liempd (2013)

Today's higher education scene is dramatically different from what it was just over a decade ago when the first edition of *The Senior International Officer (SIO) as Change Agent* appeared (Heyl, 2007). Globally, more traditional university business models have eroded; public investment in higher education, in many countries, continues to decline; and an overall negative political climate threatens the very autonomy of institutions around the world.

International higher education has not escaped the impact of these trends. Increasingly, international education is expected to pay for itself, whether this is through international student tuition, English-language training, study abroad fees, or grant funding to support new global partnerships. The result, not surprisingly, has been the increased commercialization of many international education activities (Altbach & de Wit, 2018). In addition, the widening critique of global migration patterns affects opportunities for international mobility, the lifeblood of international higher education.

This second edition both updates the themes and broadens the range of the earlier version to include selected leadership issues outside the United States, mainly from Europe, in this new context. The supporting references have likewise been expanded and updated to reflect relevant literature published since the first edition.

The authors hope that international educators everywhere will find a useful blend of theory, practice, and inspiration as they confront institutional, national, and global change in the years ahead.

I

THE BIG PICTURE

International Education in an
Age of Global Turbulence

Change comes in many forms as higher education institutions around the world operate in an increasingly turbulent and complex environment. The formidable range of issues and imperatives have been addressed by many (Altbach, 2016; Deardorff & Charles, 2018; de Wit & Altbach, in press; Hunter, de Wit, & Howard, 2016; Knight, 2015; Maringe & Foskett, 2010) and may be summed up briefly as follows.

The emergence of the global knowledge economy has placed much higher levels of expectation on universities to make a key contribution in terms of employable graduates and transferable knowledge. At the same time, the increasing integration of the world economy and the accelerated pace of change—facilitated by the explosion of new information and communication technologies— make it increasingly hard to know what will be required of people and societies in even the immediate future.

The internationalization of higher education is increasingly understood as a response to globalization, and it is becoming a strategic priority in all world regions at both national and institutional levels. While internationalization was originally based on a model of cooperation and exchange, there is now an evident shift toward a broader and more competitive understanding of internationalization, including the race for talent, international student recruitment, joint degree programs, branch campuses, and many other global initiatives that are increasingly driven more by the pressure to generate income and institutional prestige than by academic or social rationales (Altbach & de Wit, 2017; Deschamps & Lee, 2015).

There has been a significant increase in the scale and scope of international activities and operations but also an intensification of global competition, with new countries and institutions challenging the established players in the developed world. In addition, global economic and financial instability—especially the impact of the global financial crisis and economic contraction of 2007–2012—have altered and interrupted the increasingly complex flows and interactions of students and scholars. Massification, diversification, and privatization are altering the very nature of the higher education enterprise, affecting related issues of access, equality, and brain drain.

Finally, the recent wave of antiglobalization, anti-immigration, xenophobia, and other forms of populism is affecting the internationalization of higher education around the world and challenging the assumption that internationalization, in its many forms, benefits all concerned. A recent European Parliament study highlighted the following:

> We cannot ignore the fact that [the internationalization of higher education] is . . . being challenged by increasingly profound social, economic and cultural issues, such as the financial crisis, unfavorable demographic trends, immigration and ethnic and religious tensions. While these challenges represent a threat, they also raise our awareness of the importance of [internationalization] in developing a meaningful response. (de Wit, Hunter, Howard, & Egron-Polak, 2015, p. 31)

Today's international education leadership thus faces several contradictory realities. Advancing globalization continues to stimulate ever higher levels of participation in international study and exchange. But the impacts of globalization—including financial shocks, global terrorism, and growing populism—are shifting or seeking to shift institutional priorities from those of greater openness and global understanding to those of profitability and security. Let us look now at how today's senior international officer (SIO) takes on these challenges.

2

THE WORLD OF THE SIO

What Is an SIO?

In 1976, Jack Van de Water at Oregon State University may have become the first campus administrator in the United States to be named to an SIO position, that is, to an administrative role devoted full-time to international programs and initiatives (Van de Water, 2015). In this sense, the SIO role, as it is referred to in the United States, now has a history of its own.

Van de Water's initial title, *director* of a central office, reflected the early phase of campus focus on international activities. He would later be named *university dean* for international programs, reflecting the institution's commitment to anchor leadership of internationalization in the office of the chief academic officer (in the United States, that is typically associated with the role of *provost*) but with campuswide reach. Titles are not everything, but in a university setting titles and reporting lines are important, both symbolically and practically. In the decades that have followed, SIOs increasingly acquired titles farther up the campus "food chain," with many SIOs today holding titles such as vice provost, vice rector or deputy vice chancellor for international initiatives, or associate vice president or vice rector for global engagement, depending on the particular national and institutional context.

Whatever the title, the SIO designation in the United States is reserved for the person who has full-time international responsibilities and/or is the most senior campus administrator with an explicit international portfolio. The SIO position is typically an academic appointment, and the portfolio may include not only some continued teaching responsibilities but also such diverse areas as outreach, research, graduate studies, faculty development, or minority affairs.

Indeed, on some smaller campuses, the director of admissions, the chief academic officer or provost (or dean), or even the president (or rector) may de facto be the SIO.

These trends are also evident in other countries as internationalization takes on an increasingly important role within the institution. The position may be principally academic or administrative, or there may be a more distributed form of leadership in internationalization. In Europe, a range of positions may be designated as SIOs when the administrative structure is more decentralized. One commentator wrote,

> The Senior International Officer position in Europe is diverse and contextually embedded within the institutional type, size, funding model, purpose, and mission as well as the dynamic national and regional policy environment. This background shapes the specific functions and roles of the position. (Weimar, 2016, p. 41)

Whatever the institutional model, the SIO role is constantly evolving, not only in title but also in scope and function, as institutions seek to adapt to the rapidly changing challenges and opportunities of internationalization.

Why Is Leading Change a Key SIO Role?

Leading and managing change has become a hallmark of all organizational leadership in recent decades. Sometimes change is forced on organizations because of the emergence of new competitors, including those operating in a highly competitive global economy. Sometimes change is demanded by key stakeholders—governance boards or legislators—to remedy poor organizational performance or to change discredited leaders. The Internet has only accelerated this process by so quickly making organizational and leadership failures so obvious to so many. Thus, change is inevitable, even in large, established, and slow-moving organizations, like many universities.

What is different about contemporary organizational change, however, is that it is increasingly looked on by leaders not as a regrettable reality but rather as a positive good to be embraced by leadership and cultivated in organizational culture. The success of such change-agent books as *Leading Change* (Kotter, 1996), *Good to Great* (Collins, 2001), *Diagnosing and Changing Organizational Culture* (Cameron & Quinn, 2011), *Organizational Culture and Leadership* (Schein, 2010), *How to Lead* (Owen, 2011), and *A Passion for Leadership* (Gates, 2016) is a sign of the current thinking in the corporate, governmental, and nonprofit world and how they may converge. Individual leaders can make a change—a big, qualitative change—even in large and complex organizations.

Higher education leaders increasingly embrace change as well. A 2012 survey of university presidents in the United States revealed that 67% believed that either "massive" or "moderate" change was needed at their institutions (*The Chronicle of Higher Education*, 2014). Many factors provide impetus for change. These factors include the growing privatization of public higher education as governments around the world have reduced funding for public higher education and/or fostered the development of the private sector, in particular since the mid-1980s; the globalization of higher education, including the global competition for student talent; the demands of new technology in all aspects of higher education, including the dramatic growth in online education; the diversity of faculty, staff, and students, especially at public universities; the competition for enrollment at all levels; the opportunity to patent university-sponsored research discoveries or to "incubate" new companies and partner with others; and expectations of both parents and students in gaining a global perspective during university studies. In one way or another, all of these changes have implications for an institution's international engagement. It is not surprising, then, that colleges and universities have sought to strengthen, professionalize, and centralize—or in some cases broaden and decentralize—the functions of international offices in the same period. Funding has rarely kept up with campus rhetoric, but the overall direction is clear.

Campus internationalization, if it is truly an institution-wide process, presents additional change issues—and, indeed, change challenges. These will be discussed later in this monograph, but they may be summed up with one word: *silos*. As international initiatives began to be welcomed from across the institution, the question began to be asked: Who owns "international"? The question itself—the wrong question for successful internationalization—reflected the persistence of organizational silos. But some tension is inevitable as international activities begin to reach well beyond the service-oriented central office, a process increasingly referred to as *comprehensive* internationalization.

Ironically, the very success of the global agenda in recent years has forced many SIOs to wrestle with this tension in order to be effective change agents (de Wit, 2015). Writing on the context in the United Kingdom, John Taylor (2012) made an observation with which many SIOs in other countries could identify:

> On one hand internationalisation is recognised as a core function within the university with clear strategic importance; on the other hand, many staff working in the International Offices still feel themselves to be somewhat detached from the mainstream of the university. This appears to confirm the view that, in professional terms, the work of the International Office is still evolving in terms of status and recognition. (p. 9)

A recent European Association for International Education/ International Education Association of Australia (EAIE/IEAA) study (Murray, Goedegebuure, van Liempd, & Vermeulen, 2014) exploring leadership issues in Europe and Australia highlighted that internationalization activities are increasingly broadening to involve a greater number and variety of institutional players across not only teaching and research but also service functions. The survey concluded that stronger mechanisms to promote greater professionalization as well as better interaction between academic and administrative staff were imperative.

Most of the individuals selected for the SIO role in the United States, with doctoral (or other terminal) degrees in an academic discipline, have not actually studied organizational change. As with many other academic administrators, they have learned organizational leadership and management skills "on the job." Their expertise—first in a discipline, then through their international experiences or through a mix of administrative roles (the more typical route in other countries)—often has little to do with being a change agent in a broad organizational context. This speaks to the need to develop more postgraduate training and professional development for the next generation of SIOs. Future SIOs will need not only broad knowledge of the field but also the capacity for innovation and strategic and entrepreneurial skills if they are to adapt to the shifting requirements of their role (Association of International Education Administrators, 2017a; Deschamps & Lee, 2015; Charles & Pynes, 2018).

This monograph offers guidance to SIOs as they work to effect change on an institution-wide basis. It hopes to bring the issues of institutional change into even sharper focus and make them more relevant to the challenge of international education in the years to come.

3

UNDERSTANDING ORGANIZATIONS AND ORGANIZATIONAL CHANGE

Two Approaches

If SIOs are to effect sustainable, positive change in their institutions, they must acquire some knowledge about organizations in general and a much deeper knowledge about their own institution in particular. How are organizations structured? What are their internal dynamics, their "culture"? What are the levers for change? What are the barriers to change? Answers to these questions are vital for any leader devising a strategy for change.

There are many widely respected approaches to understanding organizational change. "The sheer volume of change models, case studies, and prescriptive remedies," wrote two experts in the field, "is overwhelming" (Bolman & Deal, 2013, p. 372). Two approaches are presented here because they are particularly relevant to the campus setting. Other approaches, however, are useful as well and, indeed, have helped shape these two. Which perspective SIOs prefer will depend on their work setting, theory preferences, and disciplinary background. These approaches are presented here to suggest frameworks available to SIOs to better understand their own institution and to provide guidance on initiating and sustaining change.

The Frames Approach

One approach is to see the organization—in this case a college or university—through a set of *frames*. These frames explain much about the institution and about individual leadership styles at work at one's own institution. This approach was best developed by Bolman and Deal (2013) in *Reframing Organizations: Artistry, Choice, and Leadership*. Their study has proven of such general applicability that it has been used as a core reading at Harvard University's prestigious Higher Education Institutes.

Bolman and Deal (2013) provided an analysis through which one can look at an organization from four coherent yet distinctively different perspectives. This approach can be of particular value in understanding complex organizations, as many universities and other institutions of higher education tend to be.

What are these perspectives? Bolman and Deal (2013) outlined four frames: (a) *structural*, in which rationality, appropriate goals and objectives, efficiency, and coordination are the hallmarks of the organization; (b) *human resource*, in which human needs are the guide to organizational structure, and participatory management and job enrichment reflect the commitment to put employees first; (c) *political*, in which organizations are seen as shifting coalitions of interests that inevitably come into conflict and require continuous renegotiation; and (d) *symbolic*, in which organizations are seen as "cultures, propelled by rituals, ceremonies, stories, heroes, and myths rather than by rules, policies, and managerial authority" (p. 16) (see Table 3.1).

It will be immediately apparent that in a higher education setting all four of these frames are likely to be relevant at one time or another and, in some domains of the university, possibly simultaneously. An academic dean of a large faculty may see his or her domain as best understood as political, a culture of shifting power alliances. A vice president for student affairs may see this area as requiring a human resource perspective to motivate staff to engage students and student organizations in productive ways. A vice president for finance and administration may see his or her area—indeed the entire institution—as a more or less rational structure, or at least one that must be guided by unambiguous policies and efficient coordination of roles. Unlike a corporate CEO, who may be in a position to determine the dominant frame of the organization, a college or university leader, especially in a public institution, has much

TABLE 3.1
Overview of the Four-Frame Model

	Frame			
	Structural	*Human Resource*	*Political*	*Symbolic*
Metaphor for organization	Factory or machine	Family	Jungle	Carnival, temple, theater
Central concepts	Roles, goals, policies, technology, environment	Needs, skills, relationships	Power, conflict, competition, politics	Culture, meaning, metaphor, ritual, ceremony, stories, heroes
Image of leadership	Social architecture	Empowerment	Advocacy and political savvy	Inspiration
Basic leadership challenge	Attune structure to task, technology, environment	Align organizational and human needs	Develop agenda and power base	Create faith, beauty, meaning

less leeway given the range of autonomous actors (tenured faculty, a politically appointed board of trustees, a campus workers' union, etc.) that help shape the character of the institution. The typical university president has more *legislative* than *executive* authority, although there are presidents—especially established presidents at private institutions with supportive boards—who wield considerable executive authority. The steady decline in the length of the presidential term, and the consequent shortening of the term for senior academic administrators, is yet another factor. These are everyday realities in a decentralized organization such as a higher education institution.

The point is that SIOs must understand their own institution, how key stakeholders see how the institution "works," and what frames of understanding can best guide SIOs to identify levers for change (Merkx & Nolan, 2018). The leadership skills required to initiate and sustain change will also vary within the different frames. Positive leadership skills for each frame, however, as described in Table 3.2, are not necessarily exclusive to that frame. They can in fact be useful in all frames. In contrast, the negative leadership skills

TABLE 3.2
Reframing Leadership

Frame	Leadership is effective when . . .		Leadership is ineffective when . . .	
	Leader is:	Leadership process is:	Leader is:	Leadership process is:
Structural	Analyst, architect	Analysis, design	Petty bureaucrat or tyrant	Management by detail and fiat
Human resource	Catalyst, servant	Support, empowerment	Weakling, pushover	Abdication
Political	Advocate, negotiator	Advocacy, coalition building	Con artist, thug	Manipulation, fraud
Symbolic	Prophet, poet	Inspiration, meaning-making	Fanatic, charlatan	Mirage, smoke and mirrors

described for each frame will be negative under any of the four frames.

SIOs may have a special advantage in applying Bolman and Deal's (2013) frames analysis to their context because most will bring some intercultural experience to their position. Riall Nolan, anthropologist and SIO (emeritus) at Purdue University, noted that familiarity with different cultures can help the SIO see the competing cultures of the college or university (Association of International Education Administrators [AIEA], 2017). It is not necessary to be a medieval historian, however, to appreciate Lombardi's (1991) now famous feudal metaphor to campus (especially faculty) life. Likewise, Bolman and Deal's frames can help the SIO interpret the functional meaning behind a president's rhetorical support for international initiatives (but no budgetary support) or a dean's promotion of an international program that is intended to isolate a troublesome faculty member. Promoting change can present special problems because "changing old patterns and mindsets is difficult. It is also risky" (Bolman & Deal, 2013, p. 38).

The Institutional Approach

A quite different approach to institutional change has been taken by the American Council on Education (ACE), initially through a series of publications sponsored by the Kellogg Foundation from 1998 to 2001. Under the leadership of Madeleine Green, Peter Eckel, and Barbara Hill, ACE's approach placed the process of change in an overall institutional context. Their writings were influenced by such diverse theorists as Karl Weick (1976) and John Kotter (1996). Numerous publications have followed from ACE's Center for Internationalization and Global Engagement (CIGE), including briefs, webinars, occasional papers, and the five-year *Mapping Internationalization on U.S. Campuses* (ACE, 2017b).

For ACE, change means *transformational* change toward *comprehensive* internationalization—deep, pervasive, intentional, long-term change that "alters the culture of the institution by changing underlying assumptions and overt institutional behaviors, processes, and structures" (ACE, 2001, p. 5). Moreover, such change must be based on a "strategic, coordinated process that seeks to align and integrate international policies, programs, and initiatives" (ACE, 2017a). The result is a model of internationalization that identifies six pillars required for *comprehensive* internationalization (see Figure 3.1).

ACE projects have focused more on indicators of real change and what they say about the change process than about interpreting that process. Thus, such indicators as changes in the curriculum, student learning outcomes, faculty promotion and tenure guidelines, budget priorities, and decision-making structures, along with changes in the institution's culture and self-image, are seen as keys to measuring the depth of the change. In this context, leadership, although important, is not sufficient to ensure lasting change. While acknowledging that there is no *prototype* of the successful university leader—that successful transformation is fundamentally

Figure 3.1. CIGE model for comprehensive internationalization.

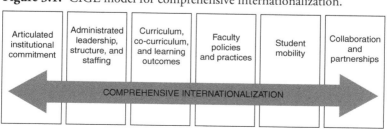

Note. Retrieved from www.acenet.edu/news-room/Pages/Center-for-Internationalization-and-Global-Engagement.aspx. Reprinted with permission of ACE.

contextual—the transforming ACE institutions do suggest that certain leadership traits are more productive than others. Winning advocates for change, creating a sense of urgency, and choosing the right agenda at the right time were all skills that mattered for successful, sustainable change.

If only indirectly, ACE brought the institutional change framework to bear on the world of the SIO. Unlike Bolman and Deal, the ACE authors emphasized what was common among institutions: a CEO (president, chancellor, rector), faculty leadership, funding issues, accreditation reviews, learning assessment, and so on. The role of the SIO, while important as an *implementer* and *coordinator* of many internationalization initiatives, is not seen as leading internationalization strategy. This was particularly apparent in ACE's recommendation that SIOs not chair (or at most cochair) a campus-wide internationalization committee (ACE, 2013). Within the institutional context, the SIO is still a *middle manager*. As Gilbert Merkx (2015), longtime SIO at the University of New Mexico and later at Duke University, noted, "Senior international officers strive to innovate, but . . . success is always contingent on the larger context and the structure of power" (p. 65).

In Europe and Australia, the aforementioned EAIE/IEAA study also identified the need for greater professionalization of internationalization leaders in the *innovator* role, but the ability to perform other roles such as *broker* and *director* was also deemed important. Brokering was seen to be increasingly crucial not only as an internal function but also an external function as relations to external stakeholder communities continued to grow and diversify. Becoming a director implied a stronger focus on skills such as strategic thinking, decisiveness, and diplomacy, as well as the ability to communicate effectively (Murray et al., 2014).

Working with different clusters of institutions focused on different but related issues—determining global learning outcomes, dealing with the new majority student, refining an institutional review process—ACE developed what it called a road map that could take an institution, of whatever mission and makeup, toward *comprehensive* internationalization. The core activity in this process has been the institutional review (Olson, Green, & Hill, 2005, pp. 15–17). The review leads to an internationalization plan that highlights student learning outcomes and thus dovetails with other unit and institutional assessments, including periodic accreditation reviews.

Finally, it must be noted that colleges and universities are notoriously change-averse institutions. As a "loosely coupled" organization (Weick, 1976), academic institutions represent a unique example of diffuse power (sometimes politely referred to as *shared governance*). Moreover, colleges and universities often combine effectively autonomous academic and administrative units, very slowly changing faculty and curriculum, and "delayed, confounded feedback" (p. 4) making it difficult to know what specific change will bring about a specific outcome (ACE, 1999). Traditional university cultures thus operate according to bureaucratic principles that place emphasis on adherence to formal procedures—resistance to a more adaptive or entrepreneurial culture can originate in perceptions that change threatens academic values and practices.

Regardless of operating cultural norms, internationalization efforts can also be easily sidelined by a lack of leadership commitment, a lack of clear strategy, or a lack of awareness among academic and administrative staff (Murray et al., 2014). "Understanding complexity—of both individual leaders and institutions," wrote Mestenhauser and Ellingboe (2005), "is . . . a typical cause of failure of educational reforms" (p. 43). Leading change of any sort, at any level, is difficult and taxing in such a setting. If one adds the financial pressures that higher education institutions are increasingly being subjected to around the world, the challenges grow significantly. Not surprisingly, change in academic institutions tends to be incremental. No wonder that the ACE authors concluded that persistence and "planning for the long-term" are keys to transformational change (ACE, 2013, pp. 11–12).

4

THE SIO AS
CHANGE AGENT

Leadership in Perspective

If one browses the "leadership" section of a large bookstore (brick-and-mortar or online), one will find dozens of "how-to" books, including *Leadership for Dummies* (Marrin, 2012). Leadership is not just for leaders anymore! Leadership within organizations has been a topic that has fascinated academics, business executives, community volunteers, politicians, and laypeople—in fact, just about everyone. The question as to why some individuals are effective in leading others and in leading organizations while others are ineffective is as old as Plato's *Republic*. In the past several decades, a wealth of literature—much of it based not only on empirical research but also on experience and intuition—has focused on organizational leadership.

This chapter provides an overview of some of the literature on organizational leadership. It is important for an SIO to have a basic working knowledge about leadership, as SIOs are usually in a (mid-level) leadership position within their institution.

Leadership in Organizations: A Theoretical Foundation

The empirical literature on leadership is quite rich. Most of the research has been done in the fields of psychology and management. The field of management, serving the for-profit sector, has been both the primary source and the primary consumer of such research. In recent years, however, a burgeoning literature has focused on the nonprofit sector. The works of Schein (2010) and Senge (2006) are examples of this literature. The guru for management literature over the past 60 years has been Peter F. Drucker (1909–2005), who was a professor of social science and management at Claremont Graduate University in California until his death.

Influenced by Drucker's work, Vandenberg, Thullen, and Fear (1986) reviewed and analyzed the literature on leadership as it applied to community-based organizations. The application of their analysis to nonhierarchical and nonprofit organizations is a useful tool for understanding some basic concepts of leadership within organizations as they apply to the SIO and the college and university settings. Each of their perspectives is described briefly in the following sections, followed by implications for the SIO.

The Trait Perspective

In this perspective, leadership is conceived of as a person's influence on a group of other people. Trait research has focused on identifying the characteristics that distinguish leaders from followers and effective leaders from ineffective leaders. Traits that have been identified by various researchers include intelligence, dominance or assertiveness, self-confidence or self-esteem, energy, task-relevant knowledge or ability or skill, and sociability. This perspective does not tell us much about distinguishing good from bad (or, as Drucker called it, *misleading*) leadership.

The Behavior Perspective

This perspective focuses on the leader's behaviors that cause certain responses in followers. Similar to that of the trait perspective, the assumption at the base of this perspective is that certain kinds of behaviors are required in all situations that enable an individual to exert leadership over others. According to Yukl (2005), these behaviors include performance emphasis, consideration, inspiration, praise recognition, structuring reward contingencies, decision participation, autonomy delegation, role clarification, goal setting, training and coaching, information dissemination, problem-solving, planning and coordinating, work facilitation, representation, interaction facilitation, conflict management, and criticism and discipline.

The Situational Contingency Perspective

From the situational contingency perspective, leadership is still viewed as influence on others, but the influence is affected by contextual factors or situational variables. Thus, leader traits and behaviors, modified by situational variables, cause certain responses in followers. Research based on this approach has aimed to discover effective leader traits and behaviors given specific situational variables. In the final ACE (2001) study on change, external pressures for change were seen as requiring leadership skills that were different from those needed when the leader had to "draw solely on internally derived energy and motivations for change" (p. 14).

The Transactional Perspective

This perspective sees the influence of leadership as a reciprocal exchange between leaders and followers (as a group). This view is essentially based on social exchange theory that focuses on the interactive process between leaders and followers. Thus, leaders' effectiveness depends on whether followers perceive them as leaders. In short, leadership is *earned* over time in respect to group expectations. This perspective places a high value on the goodwill and trust that the leader has built up over time and the kind of inspiration (even fanaticism) that followers feel from the leader's organizational and personal vision.

The Attributional Perspective

According to the attributional perspective, each individual has certain conceptions about leadership and certain expectations about how effective leaders should behave. For a leader to be considered effective, he or she must measure up to followers' perceptions of a leader. Attribution research has attempted to describe individuals' perceptions about effective leadership, the analytical process of attributing leadership to others, and the processes used by leaders when attributing follower behavior to certain causes. Thus, each individual has a personal conception of a "good" leader. In this perspective leaders can also be part of the process by determining how others conceive of being a "good" leader and thus conforming their behavior to that conception.

5

THE SIO AT WORK

Shaping an Internationalization Plan

At any given time, on any given campus around the world, some kind of strategic, or long-range, planning is going on. It may be led by the SIO, a department chair, a dean, the provost, some other vice president, the president, or even an outside professional organization or company. It may be called strategic planning and led by the division leader, or it may be assigned to a task force of faculty, staff, and students. Any new senior administrator will typically initiate some form of strategic planning within a year of assuming office.

Long-range planning creates opportunities for expanding internationalization. This is where the SIO's vision—and the compelling argument and convincing data to support it—can be helpful to increase his or her leverage as a change agent. Opportunities from various quarters to support one's own internationalization plan appear virtually on a daily basis. "The key," wrote Rumbley (2016), "is being aware of how to influence and shape future development. This requires a keen ability to understand one's context and to leverage the resources at one's disposal" (p. 4). Frankly, this is part of what makes the SIO role one of the most exciting in all of higher education.

If change is being planned in so many different parts of the college or university led by so many different people, clearly SIOs must adapt their approach to particular circumstances. This means, among other things, assessing one's personal capacities that will help determine the particular approach to change and the probable outcomes of the efforts to effect change. Understanding oneself as an administrator with key international responsibilities is a critical first step to initiating and sustaining a change process. What particular strengths and weaknesses does the SIO bring to this effort in terms of relationships to the organization and in terms of specific skills and experiences? Where can the SIO get reliable data to support his or her proposals? To whom can the SIO turn for professional advice on a controversial initiative? The goal, of course, is to take maximum advantage of one's strengths and special skills—and remedy weaknesses—in facilitating the change process.

Some call this process of self-evaluation part of the critical internal scan to determine the readiness for the kind of change the SIO seeks. Some call it knowing one's professional philosophy. It likely also involves striking an accommodation between a prior scholarly life and a newer administrative one (Scarboro, 2016). It is a combination of being grounded sufficiently in the profession of international education to know what kinds of initiatives the SIO can and cannot support and being knowledgeable about the institution to know where the real locus of power and funding lies.

The SIO brings skills and experience to bear on planning processes across the institution. Whether the role is perceived as more strategic or operational will determine the involvement of the SIO in the strategic planning process. When the SIO has direct responsibility and ownership, strategic planning will be a crucial function, but a background supportive role is also vital to the plan's success. In both cases, it requires building creative working partnerships with academic and administrative colleagues across the institution to ensure the widest possible base of support (Taylor, 2012).

Strategic Planning

Planning is an art, a science, and even a profession of sorts, with a substantial literature base, including a nomenclature and a variety of techniques and approaches. This is not the place for an extended treatment of the topic. Rather, the goal here is twofold: first, to put strategic planning in the context of the two theoretical approaches presented earlier, and second, to explore the different levels of planning on campus and the role of the SIO in each.

Planning is characterized as strategic in the sense that it offers big picture thinking and provides a meaningful sense of direction for the future. Planning—strategic or otherwise—involves developing a process for achieving certain goals and objectives. It is not surprising, then, that the first pillar of the ACE model of internationalization is an "articulated institutional commitment" to internationalization, as demonstrated in the current strategic plan (ACE, 2017a; see also Brewer, Charles, & Ferguson, 2015).

As we have seen, the most important planning often takes place early in a president's or dean's tenure. The senior academic leader may already have publicly stated the overall goals for the unit or institution, sometimes even during the hiring process or may develop the core of a strategic vision through consultation with a few senior campus leaders. The SIO should seek to be particularly active in the earliest phases of planning because it offers the greatest opportunity to shape a set of departmental, college, or even institutional goals. Building bridges early on with academic staff also helps create an understanding of the bigger picture and allows the SIO to become alert to the breadth and scale of the international endeavors under way at the institution (Proctor, 2016). There is often much more going on than the SIO knows.

Whether the SIO's contributions are bold or more cautious will depend on the leader of the unit and what his or her goals are for the planning process. Sometimes the SIO has the opportunity to articulate the international vision and goals of a dean, provost, or president. Timing is everything. The point is not to wait too long before the basic structure of the emerging plan has already been developed. Then it is probably too late to make any more than marginal changes in the plan.

Planning as Ceremony

In the context of Bolman and Deal's (2013) frames, strategic planning is seen more as an exercise to achieve a certain effect rather than a rational process that guides the future of an institution. They wrote that for many institutions, "planning is an essential ceremony that organizations stage periodically to maintain legitimacy" (p. 294). But the positive rhetoric surrounding strategic planning in the 1980s and 1990s was so pervasive that colleges and universities felt compelled to emulate what appeared to be successful techniques in the for-profit sector. Too often, however, the process became ritualistic as the university used it more to please on-campus and off-campus constituencies and support ambitious capital campaigns than to guide actual decision-making at the institution. (One aspect of university life that has used strategic planning most effectively is the so-called master plan for the campus physical environment. This "brick-and-mortar" feature of the campus, accompanied by projected real estate management, building cost estimates, and funding sources, is more likely to be pursued consistently and to be realized in practice.)

Consider, for example, the role of the SIO in the context of the frames analysis. The SIO will typically have significant responsibility (even lead responsibility) for strategic planning in the international area. This may be part of a wider strategic planning process and, not infrequently, takes place soon after a new president takes office. If the SIO assumes that strategic planning will be a rational process leading to an orderly development of short- and long-term goals, new or restructured roles, and reallocated resources leading to institutional change, he or she will likely be disappointed. This assumption holds only when a rational, structural frame best characterizes the institution. Many campus presidents state in their inaugural address what main themes they plan to emphasize, even before strategic planning has taken place. The strategic planning that follows, then, is more important for the process of engaging key campus constituents with the president's goals. Thus, strategic planning in this context is more a political and symbolic process. In the middle of a president's successful period of campus leadership, however, strategic planning may be an exercise mainly to realign roles and increase efficiency and thus best understood within a structural and human resources frame.

Like Bolman and Deal (2013), some other theorists also see planning—even strategic planning—as part of the *management* process and thus secondary to the *visioning* provided by the effective leader. "The managerial equivalent to vision creation," said Kotter (1996), "is planning" (p. 80). There is clearly a reciprocal relationship between vision setting and planning. Neither is likely to be effective alone. "Without a good vision," wrote Kotter (1996), "a clever strategy or a logical plan can rarely inspire the kind of action needed to produce major change" (p. 71). On the other hand, in a now famous phrase, "a vision without a strategy remains an illusion" (Bolman & Deal, 2013, p. 210; see also McCarthy, 2007). Figure 5.1 suggests the interconnections between leadership and management and the roles that vision, strategy, planning, and budgets play for the leader or manager.

SIO experience confirms that strategic planning at the campus level—even if it includes international goals—is rarely the "holy grail" that it appears to be. This is not to say that significant

Figure 5.1. The relationship of vision, strategies, plans, and budgets.

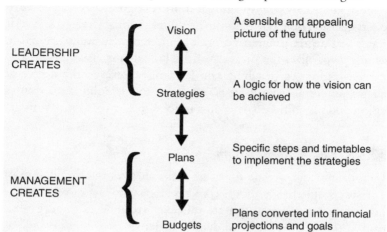

international initiatives cannot emerge from the strategic planning process. Goucher College president Sanford Ungar said that the decision in 2006 to require a study abroad experience for all Goucher College undergraduates flowed from such planning early in his presidency (Loveland, 2006). But here, too, Ungar indicated that he was already thinking about this idea during the hiring process and as he became more familiar with Goucher College's traditions and the evolving demand for global competence. Likewise, at the University of California at Davis (UC Davis), an accelerated internationalization process began in 1997 with an anguished campus indictment of UC Davis's lack of global engagement. This review led to the hiring two years later of William Lacy as vice provost for international affairs and outreach, and eventually to a Chancellor's Fall Conference (2005) focusing on international themes became part of an accelerating campuswide process. Those themes still guide the process of campus internationalization today (Lacy, 2015).

Grand plans for internationalization are rarely without controversy, as was shown by the decision in 2012 at the *Politecnico di Milano*, a technical university and public institution in Italy, to offer all postgraduate education solely in English. The vision was to transform the Politecnico from an Italian university with international students to an international university rooted in Italian tradition. Although its new English-taught programs have been highly successful, with about a third of master's students now international, strong resistance from a group of academics led to a judicial battle that has gone as far as Italy's constitutional court (Longoni, 2015). The 2018 court decision now puts Politecnico's international strategy at risk. It states that degree programs cannot be offered exclusively in English, as this jeopardizes the primacy of the Italian language and the academic freedoms of teaching and learning. However, the degree of change undertaken thus far is testimony to the Politecnico rector's vision and his ability to develop a process that enabled it to unfold.

Values, Vision, and Mission

Increasingly, the change literature sees values as the foundation of any successful change process. Values are statements of what members of an organization feel are valuable attributes of the organization, attributes that help to define it. Being "principle driven," as the ACE authors (2001, pp. 14–15) called it, was a characteristic of change leaders at the institutions that changed most significantly. Sometimes these core values are expressed in a motto, such as "Portal to New Worlds" or "Education for Social Responsibility." Mottoes such as these can provide wind behind the sails of greater internationalization. Values are thus a kind of foundation to the strategic planning process. Even though external circumstances may change, these values will remain a defining characteristic of how the institution perceives itself and wants others to perceive it. They thus provide a certain direction to where the strategic plan will be headed and, importantly, why.

Ideally, the vision that a college or university president, chancellor, or rector brings to the position articulates some aspect or aspects of the core values of the institution in a concrete time and place as projected into an ambitious but realizable future. A campus vision is fundamentally an aspiration to achieve excellence (in market terms, enhance the *brand* of the institution) in some sector (*niche*) of higher education. It is thus a crucial guide to the planning process.

The mission of the institution usually relates most closely to the original terms of its founding and to both the historic and the ongoing setting of the institution. The mission thus explains succinctly why the institution exists. The mission statement will certainly incorporate the core values of the institution and may seek to inspire as well. In addition, however, it makes more concrete the evolved role of the institution and its current purpose, including key resources and constituencies. Mission statements increasingly include the importance of preparing students for "global citizenry." Although inevitably vague, such statements are additional levers for accelerating internationalization.

Planning Assumptions

No matter what the plan—big or small, short range or long range— it is based on certain assumptions. The SIO must recognize and understand the assumptions in order to understand the plan and the planning process. Therefore, one of the first exercises in strategic planning is to review the assumptions underlying the planning process and to make them explicit. Are enrollments in higher education projected to rise or fall in the region or educational niche served by the college or university? Is the legislature (in the case of a public institution) likely to be more or less supportive of higher education? Is faculty interest in international activities growing? Are students (and their parents) likely to expect more international study options?

This process is similar to an "environmental scan," but it makes no effort to characterize these factors as "strengths" or "weaknesses." Rather, these assumptions help clarify what the environment will be in the next three, five, or however many years covered by the plan. Usually, there is no way to "prove" the accuracy of any of these assumptions, but they are a necessary context for the plan. And they can be revised in the light of objective reality as it develops. One of the great advantages for SIOs in the United States is the research of ACE staff into public-student expectations of international experiences, especially since 9/11 (ACE, 2005; Siaya, Porcelli, & Green, 2002). In the European Higher Education Area, European policies and programs for education and research are strong drivers for institutional strategies, as are increasingly national strategies for the internationalization of higher education. The latter may or may not provide funding, but when central authorities set performance targets, institutions have little choice but to take action. They are powerful levers for internationalization that the SIO can exploit.

Goals, Objectives, and Strategies

The "guts" of the strategic plan ideally emerge from a discussion— often a very broad-based and lengthy discussion—about how to achieve the vision in the context of the institution's values and mission. A wide range of approaches has been successful in this process, but change experts agree that the key to the process—even more important than specific goals or objectives in the resulting plan—is the process of engagement across the campus and beyond.

Whereas colleges and universities traditionally thought of themselves as "producing" knowledge and knowledge seekers—or at least exposing students to certain key traditions in the arts, cultures, science, and technology—today's stakeholders in higher education increasingly expect to be able to demonstrate that a certain level of learning has in fact taken place, and the assessment process focuses not only on inputs and outputs but also on learning *outcomes*.

Planning in large, complex organizations tends inevitably toward large and complex plans. The SIO should try to see that internationalization—whether that means a more internationalized curriculum, more international faculty development opportunities, more international research collaboration, or more student mobility opportunities—is integrated with the few key goals of the unit or institution. Planning is, after all, partly a mechanism for initiating creative dialogue, and the SIO's role is to inject creative, challenging ideas into that process so that internationalization is placed in the first rank of the institution's issues and concerns. At its best, strategic planning articulates a vision that can inspire and bring about change (Nolan, 2018).

Constituents, Constituencies, and Stakeholders

A college's or university's constituencies include all those individuals and groups that receive services from or are affected in any way, positively or negatively, by changes in its activities or programs—or that *perceive* themselves or their interests to be affected. They include those who can be the most vocal and effective supporters of what SIOs do and what they want to accomplish. Obvious constituencies are international students, faculty with international interests, and international alumni. A key constituency that is often overlooked is administrative staff, despite the fact that they play a key role in providing support to academic initiatives. And every institution will have its external constituencies—regional, national, and international—and a range of other possibilities from the board of trustees to the athletic program, depending on institutional circumstances.

Part of this exercise is to assess the possibilities and probabilities of success, which will obviously be better if most constituencies will benefit. It is also necessary in order to deploy information and arguments that can best persuade those not likely to support particular changes. And it is also crucial in devising the political strategy for carrying out the change agenda. Who will be allies? Who will be critics? And how can the SIO persuade the key constituencies to be supportive?

Because constituents are important to any agenda, it is important to identify them, communicate with them effectively, and even organize them in support of the international agenda. At every opportunity, the SIO should convert them into stakeholders. One way of doing this is to seek to understand their priorities and the interest or influence they may or may not have in internationalization. A good way to start is by asking these constituents their opinions, the first step in building a successful relationship (Merkx & Nolan, 2018, pp. 49–50).

Another way to convert constituents into stakeholders is to feature them in publications the SIO issues from the international office. Strategic commissioning and placement of articles featuring academic units launching new international initiatives—such as international students in public health or a new research collaboration in engineering—can build dialogue with new campus players. Before long, this kind of encouragement can lead to articles written by faculty on their summer study abroad programs in the student newspaper or faculty weekly. Likewise, UC Davis's *Internationally Engaged*, a semiannual publication, gave SIO Lacy a voice to promote new initiatives of his office and to showcase international activities from a wide range of academic units. Lacy (2015) recalled, "This helped strengthen our collaborations across the entire campus" (p. 194).

Douglas Proctor (2016), director of international affairs at University College Dublin (Ireland), recognized that it was only when he moved up the ranks and took on a senior management position in internationalization—where he worked on a daily basis with academic staff to not only shape institutional strategy but also achieve outcomes—that he "became truly alert to the breadth and scale of international academic endeavours" (p. 19) at his university. He also reflected on the rigid silos within academic institutions that often prevent SIOs from seeing their work as part of a broader institutional agenda for internationalization.

The challenges—and opportunities—in overcoming institutional silos are echoed by another Irish colleague. Erin Paullin (2016), global officer at Trinity College Dublin, explained how the university has introduced school-based global officers entrusted with implementing a global relations strategy on a micro scale as they work with the different schools to develop and deliver their own international strategies in line with the university's broader global strategy. She highlighted the role of each global officer as varied, complex, and dependent on the needs of the different schools. For "many of the schools," she added, "it is a new departure to have an administrative staff role integrated within their school that is specific to the development and integration of international activities" (p. 11). One of the positive outcomes of this new role is that the schools feel more connected to the institutional strategy because there are now stronger communication lines between the different levels and between faculty, administrators, and students. Internationalization efforts are now more "effective, integrated, and accessible" (Paullin, 2016, p. 11), which has to be good news.

Interaction must go both ways. Just as individual schools and faculties are developing their own international agendas—and their own global officers—the SIO must seek face-to-face contact with potential stakeholders both on campus and abroad to build the kind of trust, support, and common interest that is required when the time comes to act on the change agenda. Having regular visits with deans, being actively involved in area study clusters of faculty, and even meeting with entire departments to explain the functions of the international office can both acknowledge the contributions of faculty and academic administrators and gain valuable feedback on the core services of the office. This is the "reflective conversation" that many SIOs subscribe to as a critical vehicle for change (Nolan & Hunter, 2012, p. 132). Jack Van de Water (2000), the second president of the AIEA (1985–1986), put this most tellingly and succinctly: "You will not succeed if you stay in your office" (p. 32).

Sounding Boards

Open and candid feedback on international initiatives is indispensable to the SIO attempting programmatic innovation. Usually this takes the form of an internal body appointed by the senior academic officer and chaired by a faculty member—or cochaired with the SIO. This group is called the Council on International Initiatives at the University of Missouri–Columbia, the International Education Committee at Grand Valley State University, the International

Studies Advisory Committee at Murray State University, and the International Programs and Services Advisory Committee at the University of the Pacific. Whatever the name, the important feature of the group is that it truly represents all large academic units (colleges, faculties, or divisions), with faculty representation that has the confidence of the deans. Key administrative units (graduate programs, library, campus technology, etc.) and student representation are common features of such groups.

Each institution will define the membership of its own international committee according to the role it sees the committee playing. Fielden (2012) suggested that it might have a more strategic role with a small number of high-level members. If the committee plays a more managerial role of coordinating and driving forward the internationalization agenda, it will need to include a larger representation of the faculties and departments involved. Still another option is to orient the committee more for information exchange and coordination among all the managers involved, rather than for a focus on decision-making. Fielden concluded that several mechanisms might need to be established to oversee a comprehensive internationalization strategy.

External advisory councils are also helpful in broadening the circle of stakeholders. Some external advisory bodies include an explicit fundraising responsibility for international initiatives. Whatever the structure of such groups, they should be used meaningfully and their advice seriously considered. Nothing is more counterproductive, especially for CEO-level and other busy people, than a purposeless and time-consuming exercise of information sharing without the opportunity to be involved in impactful innovation. Following its participation in ACE's Internationalization Laboratory in 2010–2011, Case Western Reserve University (CWRU; Cleveland, Ohio) launched a "visiting committee" that brought together two dozen (mainly) CWRU alumni with wide-ranging international expertise and leadership credentials to recommend policy initiatives to the campus (ACE, 2013).

International advisory boards have typically been set up in universities seeking to enhance their status and global reputation. The recent growth in national excellence initiatives around the world—such as in China, France, Germany, the Russian Federation, Spain, and South Korea—has also seen the development of such boards as a means to access international expertise that can help benchmark the institution internationally (Altbach, Mihut, & Salmi, 2016).

In 2017, the University of Granada (Spain) set up an International Advisory Board with a broader perspective, one that could enhance the quality of the internationalization process for all involved. Dorothy Kelly (personal communication, February 16, 2018), vice rector for internationalization, said that the five members were chosen because of their range of experience in Europe, Latin America, the Mediterranean area, and the developing world. They will offer expertise in a range of areas including mobility, internationalization of the curriculum, language policy, doctoral education, development cooperation, and governance issues. In addition to meeting with senior management, board members will engage with staff and students to help take stock of progress and advise on areas for improvement. Their presence in the institution will also offer an opportunity to raise awareness through lectures, seminars, and informal networking events.

Assessment and Continuous Learning

The pace of change—in technology, in the global economy, and in society at large—is such that universities are called on to be continuous learning organizations. As President Peter McPherson said in a 1994 address at Michigan State University, "Globalization is causing a rapid and continuous restructuring. No organization can ignore this cascade of changes. Those universities that stay ahead of the curve will be among the successful" (p. 6). This observation was made at the dawn of the Internet age; it is clearly even truer today.

Assessing progress toward explicit goals can assist the university in constantly renewing its human capital, which is key to confronting the "cascade of changes" of the twenty-first century. For this reason, every college or university must become a *learning organization* in both senses of the term (Deardorff, 2018). It goes without saying that the campus is about learning: faculty and students who extend the boundaries of knowledge. But too few campuses are true *learning organizations* in Peter Senge's (2006) sense of the term: an organization that continually learns to fulfill its mission in more effective ways. SIOs can make a unique contribution to both meanings of the term because they participate in a unique global network that can keep the campus informed on leading trends in global education. These trends are themselves harbingers of even bigger trends in the global economy and global security.

In this context, the strategic plan—at whatever level—should be regarded as a living, evolving document providing as clear a sense of direction for the organization as possible for a given time period. The strategic plan is not a set of immutable principles (aside from the statement of values and mission that may, indeed, be intended as permanent), and it can serve the organization only if it reflects consensus within the organization and the realities and circumstances of time and place.

Periodically reviewing, updating, and revising the strategic plan gives it life and meaning for the organization. Usually, this review is done on a three- or five-year cycle. (Annual reviews should be limited in scope, lest the process become too bureaucratic and focused on short-term performance.) Revisions should be based on the assessment of the current plan's performance in meeting its goals and objectives. For example, the University of the Pacific's "Pacific 2020," adopted in 2012, was "refreshed" in 2016 as "Pacific 2020R" (University of the Pacific, 2018). One of the outcomes was a reorganization of international services at the university. This is a crucial cycle within a cycle. Past performance is used to determine any changes in direction or activity for the future. Assessment, in other words, is the principal process guiding the regular review and revision—and ensuring accountability—of the strategic plan.

Internationalization Plans

Planning for greater internationalization takes place at several levels in any institution; the larger and more complex the campus, the more diverse the planning. In this sense there are often several international plans in the process of development at any given time. The general themes noted previously apply to each of these plans, but the role of the SIO varies substantially among them.

Despite some skepticism about the relevance of institutional strategic planning, there is no doubt that experienced SIOs consider skills in strategic planning to be essential for the effective conduct of their work (Association of International Education Administrators, 2015). The prevalence of conference sessions and preconference workshops on strategic planning at professional meetings also suggests that strategic planning is seen as very important from the point of view of the SIO. And there are indeed two other levels of strategic planning that are accessible to the SIO and may be as promising as the institutional planning process discussed earlier.

The first level of strategic planning that is most under the direct control of the SIO is planning within the international office or whatever portfolio is included under the SIO role on campus. The goal is obviously to provide a seamless array of services to the campus, faculty, staff, and students. This is fundamentally a support function. But here too SIOs can markedly increase their influence on broader campus internationalization by leading an effective office that delivers high-quality and consistent service to others. Planning that responds to the needs of the core clients of the office is often the most effective. For this reason, continuous surveying—both formal and informal—of the responses to the services of the office is particularly important. How can the turnaround time for key documents for international students be improved? How can promotion of international study options be strengthened by collaborating with faculty and lead administrators in key departments? How can matching funding with deans expand the pool of resources for internationalization? What new services would improve the perception and influence of the office on campus?

Planning for these *qualitative* outcomes often has to take place alongside (even outside) the continuing demands for *quantitative* indicators. It has often been noted that this kind of planning for day-to-day administrative work is rarely part of the professional preparation of the SIO. Clearly planning at the unit level requires both advocating for programmatic innovation and delivering measurable outcomes.

The second level of strategic planning that offers promising opportunities for internationalization is the planning that goes on in one of the other academic or administrative units on a virtually continuous basis. This requires outreach to other parts of the campus. Can the campus career center be interested in helping to develop (and fund) international internships? Can the women's center integrate international women students into its leadership programming? Can the health sciences faculty develop international study programs for graduate students in the developing world?

There are many paths to greater integration of the international office with diverse campus units. Serendipity certainly plays a part in this kind of collaboration, but planning can make it more likely and more sustainable. Becoming part of another unit's strategic plan can be the surest route to broader internationalization.

Yulia Grinkevich, director of internationalization, and Maria Shabanova, deputy director of the Academic Integration Centre, Office of Internationalisation at National Research University Higher School of Economics in Moscow (Russia), reflected on how decentralization of traditional functions of the international office has led to a greater need for integration of internationalization into the work of other academic or administrative units. Whether a centralized or decentralized approach is chosen, each structural change requires SIOs to rethink how they work with other units in order to ensure internationalization is successfully embedded across campus. They highlighted the need for both professional competence and an ability to innovate and integrate. They concluded, "It is vital that . . . [SIOs] remain in the loop about the university's strategy and how their work relates to it—aware of the internal and external contexts" (Grinkevich & Shabanova, 2016, p. 7).

Each institution, depending on a range of different factors such as history, size, external circumstances, and the extent of its international activities, will determine whether to develop a single comprehensive institutional strategy or a separate plan for internationalization. Whatever the approach, it is fundamental that internationalization be embedded in institutional activities and understood as a cross-functional dimension. Placing internationalization within the wider context of the institutional strategic plan—with a series of supporting actions—gives it real meaning and enhances its role and value (Hunter & Sparnon, 2018).

Comprehensive Internationalization

Increasingly, colleges and universities are launching planning processes that focus on the internationalization of the campus. Here, obviously, the SIO should play a key role, providing relevant data, historical perspective, opportunities for external funding, and a sense of opportunity for the future. ACE's institutional review was developed as part of or as a prelude to this sort of strategic planning for internationalization.

The stimulus for shaping a campuswide internationalization plan may come from outside the institution or from the decision to hire an outside consultant to assess the prospects for accelerated internationalization. This kind of decision may be the basis for an institutional review that is the centerpiece of the ACE process discussed previously. This can emerge predictably when the international office, along with other comparable middle management units, is up for its five-year unit review. Or this can occur in reaction to a key retirement or departure among internationally focused administrative positions and in anticipation of hiring replacement staff.

The motivation behind the comprehensive review is important: The higher the administrative initiator of the review and the more urgent the context of the review, usually the more significant the results and the more likely the results will be implemented. For example, at Wake Forest University, SIO Pia Wood played a key role in shaping the Quality Enhancement Program (QEP) required by the university's accreditation visit in 2006. This external review provided the impetus to put internationalization high on the campus agenda and helped create an ambitious and detailed plan for a comprehensive process.

The ACE authors have promoted an integrative approach to internationalization that goes beyond planning for a range of international activities to include both a systematic institutional review and an assessment of global learning outcomes. This dual approach challenges institutions to assess (measure) student progress toward learning a predetermined set of knowledge, skills, and attitudes. Inevitably, this approach requires an inclusive campus process, because assessing learning outcomes means not merely enhancing and aligning campus activities but working with departments on the intersection among general education, global education, and specific majors (Olson et al., 2005).

Clearly the SIO plays an important role in this review and planning process, perhaps even a lead role. This approach is highly relevant to SIOs because their areas of responsibility—education abroad, language across the curriculum, international internships, international students (especially research-relevant graduate students), international faculty development, and international campus programming—impinge directly or indirectly on the quality of the campus product. Moreover, they have access to cross-disciplinary and cross-divisional data that can be particularly illuminating. To be sure, this is mostly *input* data. For example, how many international students are enrolled in each college? Or how many courses in a given department have significant international content? How many students study abroad by college and major? How many faculty are involved in active international linkages? Supplying these data not only provides various benchmarks for a future internationalization plan but also challenges other key partners to develop comparable *outcome* measures. "Assessment is hard work," wrote Deardorff and van Gaalen (2012), "but well worth the investment in determining the impact of institutions on student learning and in preparing students for the global world in which they live and work" (p. 187).

Internationalization of the Curriculum and Internationalization at Home

One measure of the growing importance of global issues on campus is that both senior administrators and SIOs are recognizing that the curriculum is the linchpin for comprehensive internationalization. As has often been observed, students graduate, faculty retire, administrators move on—but the curriculum endures.

Globalization and Curricular Reform

The SIO can rarely play a lead role in this process of curricular reform except when the SIO is at the same time a regular faculty member. But regardless of their role in the process, SIOs can take advantage of a number of levers for change (Leask & Charles, 2018). Professional accreditation associations, for example, in business, engineering, and education, have included global competence themes in their standards for the curriculum. Moreover, some disciplines themselves have worked out at least general frameworks for assessing global knowledge and skills (Green & Schoenberg, 2006). As part of their participation in the Global Learning for All project, ACE partner institutions have developed global learning outcomes at representative research universities, liberal arts colleges, and community colleges (Olson et al., 2005). For the SIO, there is no substitute for a respected, internationally experienced faculty member who will lead the effort to review the curriculum with a charge to strengthen existing international components, introduce new ones, and propose global learning assessment measures. The SIO can facilitate these processes, for example, by simply requesting a report on departmental or college curricular contributions to campus internationalization.

Moreover, the process of globalization itself has clear implications for the college and university curriculum. The most common university response has been to add a course or two on globalization—most likely in the social sciences or business. A stronger response has been to develop new majors, minors, or certificates. But however successful in terms of faculty commitment and student enrollment, these initiatives all represent limited approaches to general education in a global era. Can more be done?

SIOs can leverage their knowledge of the globalization process to help shape curricular reform. In a little-cited concluding section to *The Lexus and the Olive Tree*, Friedman (1999) proposed a *rapid change opportunity act* to deal with the human displacement that globalization inevitably creates. For higher education, doesn't this process call for a *rapid change curriculum*? If so, what should this curriculum look like? How does it converge with other models of higher education?

Globalization poses—or at least supports and helps frame—the enduring critical thinking goals that all educators hope to develop in their students. It raises such questions as the following: How do we measure change in human affairs? What are guides for ethical action in a global age? How can we understand and help solve global inequities and global problems—all of which are interdisciplinary, transnational, and culturally sensitive? The responses to these questions could be formulated as benchmark courses, seminars, or competencies in a globally focused curriculum. SIOs should try to leverage these teachable moments—which they confront more directly and more consistently than most of their colleagues—to encourage a new kind of global learning at the center of a student's higher education journey (Brewer & Cunningham, 2009; Brewer & Leask, 2012; Leask & Charles, 2018).

The Curriculum and Beyond

Outside the United States, the terms *Internationalization of the Curriculum* (IoC) and *Internationalization at Home* (IaH) are more commonly used when discussing this topic. IaH developed as a concept in Europe in an attempt to provide an international dimension to the learning experience of nonmobile students, whereas IoC was used more often in Australia and the United Kingdom. Beelen and Jones (2015) argued that IoC encompasses IaH, but while IoC includes outbound mobility programs, IaH focuses exclusively on the home university and its surrounding environment.

Beelen and Jones (2015) described what IaH and IoC have in common and also cleared up some misconceptions regarding what is needed to internationalize the curriculum or the home campus. Both IoC and IaH aim to reach 100% of students, share an intercultural and international focus, are embedded in the curriculum and the cocurriculum, are delivered through internationalized learning outcomes and assessment, and are specific to different programs of study. Moreover, neither is dependent on the presence of international students or staff, nor do they assume that such presence will lead to "automatic internationalization" (Beelen & Jones, 2015, p. 8). Neither requires a curriculum taught in English (Beelen & Jones, 2015).

Both IaH and IoC are increasingly declared to be important elements of a broader and more purposeful approach to internationalization. In Europe, the *EAIE Barometer* revealed that 50% of universities have IaH in their plans for internationalization, while the International University Association's *Trends 2015* survey showed 64% embracing IaH activities (Beelen & Jones, 2015). What is actually happening is less known, but regardless of the level or degree of involvement of SIOs in IaH or IoC, authentic curricular change will happen only if academics are fully engaged in the process. This is not a change that can happen overnight.

However, Leask, Green, and Whitsed (2015), who have carried out extensive research and professional development on IoC in Australia, indicated ways in which this change can be carried out collaboratively and lead to meaningful transformation. They stated that the challenge is not about convincing academics of the need to rethink the curriculum. They already understand that their students need and want to be able to live and work effectively in a globalized world.

The challenge is that many academics do not know how to integrate international skills into their course work. Leask and colleagues (2015) proposed that any change process must first start with a discussion about why it is important in the respective disciplines and reach a point of agreement before approaching the important stage of describing the learning outcomes. This is not an easy process. The authors encouraged a campus conversation among the different disciplines to learn from one another and exchange best practices. Beyond what insights SIOs might offer on specific courses, there is clearly a role the SIO can play in coordinating such initiatives within "institution-wide, integrated, intentional, and visible internationalization strategies" (Leask et al., 2015, p. 35).

6

THE SIO AT WORK

From Planning to Implementation

An improved process is not a substitute for an improved outcome. As former Intuit CEO Steve Bennett noted, "Process is an enabler to achieve an outcome; it is not the desired outcome" (Vara, 2007, p. R3). Likewise, planning does not ensure a different outcome. The spirit behind the new (or renewed) process of global engagement, encouraged from above and supported by other faculty and administrative units, is the key to success in this area.

Reviewing current campus practices regarding international education and preparing an internationalization plan and making transformational change are very different things. How can the SIO find the *flywheel*—to use Collins's (2001, pp. 164–178; 2005, pp. 23–28) term—in the process of comprehensive internationalization? JoAnn McCarthy (2007), former assistant provost for international affairs at the University of Pennsylvania (and AIEA president, 2001–2002), wrote,

> Whether the institution is large, small, public, private, urban, or rural, successful internationalization will flow from its core values and mission. An internationalization plan that resonates with faculty members, administrators, students, alumni, and trustees will be in sync with the past and, at the same time, inspire new visions of the future. It will take the institution's basic identity and project it onto a global stage. (p. B12)

This chapter provides a perspective on SIOs as leaders of change within their institutions. It will use some, though not all, of the concepts described in the previous chapters. The views about the SIO as a leader for change described in the following sections are based more on experience than on theory, but the two often illuminate one another.

Three Change Agent Values

Just as senior university leaders have their own agenda when they take office, the SIO should likewise develop a set of goals soon after assuming the role. Basically, the highly effective SIO must be passionately committed to three propositions:

1. International education, in its various forms, is a vital component of university-level learning and experience in the twenty-first century.
2. The SIO's goal is to move the internationalization of the entire institution forward and to move the international dimension from the periphery to the core of the institution, not just the office or administrative unit he or she directs.
3. The process of change must be open and transparent, with periodic assessment relevant to comprehensive internationalization available to all.

These three commitments combine the passion for change with the focus on the larger goal and a transparent process. When all three commitments are actualized and working together for maximum effectiveness, the SIO achieves what Collins called "Level 5 Leadership" (2001, pp. 17–40; 2005, pp. 9–13). This is obviously rarely the case—or perhaps achieved only episodically in the course of an SIO's career, at the right institution with the right senior leadership—but it should be the ever-present goal.

Three Change Agent Realities

Three realities inevitably constrain the SIO's leverage for becoming an institutional change agent. First, as noted earlier, colleges and universities are notoriously decentralized ("loosely coupled" [Weick, 1976]), conservative organizations. Just as this reality circumscribes the direct authority of the campus president, it even more sharply delimits the official authority of SIOs, especially outside their own reporting line. As has been noted at several points in this monograph, SIOs often find their room for leadership constrained by the walls of one of the several campus silos. Second, the international education agenda of the institution, if indeed it has been formulated, is bound to be somewhere on the periphery of a few core missions. Third, the SIO is frequently the director of an administrative unit (the "international office"), with demanding management responsibilities and a budget based on funding administrative functions and often providing little truly discretionary monies (Schlör & Barnes, 2012). The more time SIOs spend managing office staff, the less time they have available to provide leadership to campuswide internationalization. Successful change agent SIOs tend to have a mix of experienced senior staff with long institutional tenure and newer hires that buy into the change agenda.

All of these constraints can be overcome or at least reduced. Indeed, one could just as well point to several trends that are bound to be supportive of internationalization in higher education. For one thing, the expectations of parents for more effective global education for their children entering higher education continues to run well ahead of the delivery of that education during the student experience in many parts of the world. Second, students—in part as a result of globalization and the rise of global terrorism—are increasingly interested in international subjects. In the United States, international studies and international business are among the largest majors on many campuses; international study, while still involving only a small percentage of college students, has risen by almost 50% in the past decade (Institute of International Education, 2018). Third, as many commuter, urban, and rural campuses in the United States become more residential, the interest in international and intercultural activities (including international study) will likely increase as well.

Similar trends are emerging in countries all around the world. As has already been noted, however, countertrends including antiglobalization have been gaining traction in many countries. Any change process that seeks to promote internationalization as a means to enhance the quality of an institution's academic programs must also think carefully about how it will affect, and contribute to, the society in which the university or college is located. This is no longer simply a desirable outcome; it is a strategic imperative.

Coalition Building

Coalition building, campus networking, and cross-disciplinary communication have all been mentioned earlier in this monograph. But they deserve repeating. The key to being an effective SIO is developing coalitions that support creative ideas that in turn support key elements of the international agenda as part of a larger goal. The most obvious partners in this process are academic deans, but others as far afield as campus housing, financial aid, and alumni relations may also be important. In fact, the entire campus should be seen as a potential partner in campus internationalization. A strategic approach to internationalization recognizes the value of administrative staff as equal partners and actively builds on their involvement (Hunter, 2018). As Van de Water (2000) pointed out long ago, "By creating an environment where good ideas are surfaced, brokered, encouraged, leveraged, and implemented within a partnership framework, the central office is providing leadership, gaining influence, and serving as an effective change agent" (p. 37).

Honor the past; challenge the future. Nothing alienates campus partners more than to be told that the way things were done in the past were ill advised, badly managed, or incompetently executed. The SIO inevitably comes into the stream of internationalization somewhere along the way. (Even at new institutions, the faculty, staff, and students immediately bring international experience to the campus.) Therefore, one must strike a balance between acknowledging the past contributions of faculty and staff and challenging them to reach higher.

Recognize partners. One of the areas in which an SIO typically has considerable freedom is in recognition activities. Most offices hold some form of annual recognition event. The goal of the SIO should be to raise the prestige of this recognition with awards consistent with institutional practice and at the level of other campus recognition. Ideally, a faculty award, for example, should be made at an annual faculty awards ceremony—in addition to whatever office-sponsored event the SIO may arrange. A staff award might include a gift certificate at a local retailer. A student award might include a copy of a current book on globalization. Partners can never be thanked enough.

A Continuous Process

The SIO can usefully think of the challenge of internationalization—indeed as any change process—as an iterative process that

regularly doubles back on itself as circumstances change. It is iterative because the very nature and scope of campus internationalization needs to be refined (perhaps even reinvented) as the process
accelerates.

To be successful, the SIO must possess the experience, skills,
and will to continuously lead or facilitate this process. The administrator must see himself or herself as a future-oriented visionary,
not necessarily adding more rhetoric to the campus dialogue—some
would say that there is already too much international rhetoric on
campus—but rather helping the campus see its future identity with
a clearly defined international dimension.

The pace of change at the beginning of the twenty-first century is such that, as with business enterprises, colleges and universities must be nimble enough to define themselves as *international*
institutions in ways that are credible, sustainable, and true to the
institution's fundamental character. This matrix of entrepreneur-
ship, global forces, and institutional culture provides the creative
environment in which SIOs work and thrive today.

International Education Ethics

There are ethical issues here, of course. As with any human endeavor,
openness and a sense of standards in dealing with others is the only
assurance of ultimate satisfaction with one's work. Even a strong
ethical basis, however, does not guarantee success as a change agent.
NAFSA's Code of Ethics (www.nafsa.org) continues to evolve and
provides a sound basis for most gray areas in international education. Other statements on ethical practice include AIEA's Standards
of Professional Practice for International Education Leaders and
Senior International Officers (www.aieaworld.org); the Best
Practices statement by the American International Recruitment
Council (www.airc-education.org); and those identified in the
European Association for International Education's International
Student Mobility Charter (www.eaie.org), in the Canadian Bureau
for International Education's Code of Ethical Practice (www.cbie
.ca), in the Forum on Education Abroad's Code of Ethics (www
.forumea.org), and in the International Association of Universities'
Call for Action Affirming Academic Values in Internationalization
of Higher Education (www.iau-aiu.net).

Inevitably, however, issues arise that raise troublesome questions: Should a dean proceed with a linkage abroad funded by an

international partner who won't reveal the sources of the program funding? Can international student offices require that students purchase health insurance from a single vendor? Should study abroad offices accept rebates for enrolling students with certain program providers? And with the increasing global competition for qualified international students, should universities pay recruiters "by the head" for enrolled students? And at the macro level, what impact do SIO decisions have on access and equality for students and scholars from institutional partners and around the globe (Deardorff, Rosenbaum, & Teekens, 2018)? Change often creates new contexts in which these ethical choices must be made. It is part of the change agent's responsibility to try to foresee such situations and develop an institutional consensus on appropriate guidelines for practice.

Gauging the Institution's Readiness for Change

As noted earlier, the first step in implementing change is to understand how the institution works. This is itself an ongoing exercise, because new senior administrators can, over time, make substantial changes to how an institution functions. What are the kinds of interactions, partnerships, and teamwork that will support the internationalization of the institution? Through what frames is the institution best understood? Is the institution readying itself for transformational change?

As a change agent, the SIO must understand the levers for change on campus. What levers are directly available to the SIO will depend in part on the authority vested in the SIO position itself. Although an increasing number of campuses are naming SIOs at the vice president, vice provost, or vice rector level, in most institutions SIOs are at the dean or director level and are thus, as noted earlier, part of the diverse middle management of the institution. These positions inevitably involve working daily with myriad on-campus and even off-campus partners.

Whatever position the SIO occupies on campus, he or she reports directly or indirectly to some vice president. That vice president also has a set of priorities that will likely place international education in a second or third tier. New chief academic officers, for example, must first identify the priorities of the president. Presidents often come to their CEO position with an academic agenda of their own. Second, chief academic officers must identify and cultivate faculty leaders who will be key partners in any change agenda. Third, new chief academic officers may well have to organize (or reorganize) their office staff. These priorities may well dominate the thinking of these leaders for the first year or two of their tenure. The SIO must respect these priorities while finding ways to show that strengthening international education is itself supportive of these priorities.

SIO positions are commonly found on organizational charts in campus phone directories, in college bulletins, and certainly in international documents. These charts still look basically hierarchical, dominated by the great campus silos of academic affairs (and the variety of academic colleges or schools), student affairs, administrative services, and fund-raising. Such charts are increasingly anachronistic, as creative business management either does away with such charts completely or reinvents them to keep creative and productive human resources flowing to greatest effect. Thinking only in terms of these vertical silos found on all campuses is a fundamental obstacle to comprehensive campus internationalization.

Instead, the effective SIO builds another organizational matrix in his or her mind, one quite different from the one found in official organization charts. This matrix is more interactive, dynamic, and interdependent (like the global economy itself!) and places internationalization at the *center* of the design, not on the periphery. Such a design might be as simple as a series of concentric circles with the president and chief academic officer at the center, the international office and the campuswide international advisory body in the next ring, followed by a ring of deans, and projecting out to the edges of the circular pattern (and beyond) with special programs (area studies, internships, exchange programs, speaker series, etc.) that illustrate the signature international activities of the different colleges and schools. In this virtual schema, there would be lots of arrows at various intermediary rings that suggest the interaction of the different units: alumni relations linking to an endowed global lectureship, the study abroad office linking to faculty development, and so on. The design—never finished, always evolving—might look fairly neat and symmetrical or be a more fanciful creation. The evolution of the design should be presented regularly to international office staff to help them understand and appreciate their growing influence on campus. In time, effective SIOs find that other partners seek to be part of the *internationalization* chart, rather than simply the organizational chart of the campus.

The work of the SIO is inherently multi- and interdisciplinary because cross-cultural communication and the great twenty-first-century real-world issues are multi- and interdisciplinary. Coalition building across reporting lines is the SIO's modus operandi, because there are internationally experienced and internationally "ready" resources in all parts of the campus. For example, on some campuses the most developed student-life research capacity rests in student affairs. This capacity can present current student data that measures progress toward a truly international ethos on campus or toward the broad impact of an internationalized curriculum. On such campuses, the SIO in academic affairs must be able to pull on that lever for change. On some campuses, development and alumni relations may include a fund-raiser who is internationally active and committed. Here is a lever for change in such areas as recruiting international students, funding international endowment priorities, and enhancing campus–corporate linkages on international projects. An internationally motivated faculty member may be interested in transforming a traditional physical education department into more of a tourism and leisure studies department—thus opening doors for global engagement.

In a word, the SIO must think *ecologically*. And the ecology goes well beyond the campus itself. The SIO must also act *opportunistically*. Gabara (2015) told the story of a colleague calling her "opportunistic"—and "my Central European soul crumbled in horror" (p. 136). Subsequently, she learned that taking advantage of rare opportunities to advance campus internationalization is a positively good thing. The truth is SIOs can achieve extraordinary things, even things not in the strategic plan, when they are attuned to promising surprises that come their way. On campus, administrators and their staffs enjoy interacting with faculty when they feel they are working together on a joint project to which senior academic leaders are committed. And faculty enjoy working with faculty from other disciplines with common interests. The trick is to pull together these coalitions to benefit from the joys of creative—and sometimes unplanned and unexpected—international teamwork (Merkx & Nolan, 2018).

An example that reveals the long-term sustainability of collaboration is the Global Scholars Program at the University of Missouri–Columbia (MU, 2018). The idea for the program—a faculty development travel program focusing on transitional societies and economies—began in a brainstorming session with the campuswide international advisory body in 1997 and turned into a grant proposal to the U.S. Department of Education's (USDOE's) International Studies and Foreign Language (Title VI) grant program. The program began with a combination of summer travel programs, individual curriculum projects, and campus workshops on internationalizing the undergraduate curriculum. As of 2016, more than 200 faculty had participated in the activities of the Global Scholars Program, and many thousands of students have been affected by the new and revised courses. A total of 26 different countries have been visited as part of group summer seminars, and all academic divisions of the university (including university libraries) have participated (with arts and sciences, journalism, and health sending almost 40% of the participants) through either group or individual projects.

Following three years of United States Department of Education support, the program became a budgeted activity managed by the international center and funded by the provost office. In 2002, the Institute of International Education (IIE) recognized the program with an Andrew Heiskell Award for Innovation in International Education. In fact, the Missouri program, although innovative in its institutional context at the time, was very similar to Richmond's Faculty Seminar Abroad Program (Gabara, 2015) begun already in 1989 and one at UC Davis that began in 2000 (Lacy, 2015).

Missouri's Global Scholars Program has evolved significantly over the years and now serves newly identified goals for MU's internationalization. The international center has had three directors and the campus has had six chancellors (including interim chancellors) and five provosts (including interim provosts) since the inception of the program. The durability of the program, however, reflects the roles that an innovative idea, a receptive institutional context, and leadership play in sustained organizational change. As a veteran SIO observed, "Institutionalization, not innovation, is the hallmark of real change" (Nolan, 2015, p. 182).

This kind of campus-based program represents a combination of Collins's "hedgehog" and "fox" styles of leadership (Collins, 2001, pp. 90–119; 2005, pp. 17–23). SIOs probably cannot change their basic propensity for hedgehog thinking (focused, single-minded, persistent) or fox thinking (scattered, brilliant, mercurial). But over time, SIOs can learn to balance these qualities, sometimes with the help of partners who bring the other style to the partnership. And SIOs, like all university administrators, can grow and evolve into effective "leader-manager" change agents.

Shaping the Institution's International Identity

What kind of international education will the institution offer in the next 10 to 20 years? The prior question, of course, is, What kind of overall educational opportunities will the institution offer to the next generation? Colleges and universities are right now educating the citizens, neighbors, coworkers, and leaders of the first half of the twenty-first century. Can anyone doubt that this period will require more global knowledge, more global thinking, and more cross-cultural insights than ever before? SIOs as change agents must be able to help institutions articulate an international vision and identity that addresses these needs.

What do we mean by *international identity?* There are too many dimensions and too many creative international opportunities for any single college or university to be "doing it all." Different institutions will have different international identities. Flagship research universities may choose to emphasize faculty research collaboration leading to the incubation of new technologies and technical assistance globally. Regional universities may emphasize area study programs, international service-learning, and "internationalization at home" through globally oriented residential colleges. A small, private university may emphasize a highly international general education curriculum required of all students and international study accessible to all students. There is no single formula for internationalization that is applicable to all institutions. Context and campus culture are crucial factors.

The role of the SIO is to help colleagues articulate an international identity that is credible and sustainable. Sometimes this comes in the form of a few key questions: What counts as a significant international experience for students at this institution? How does that experience relate to other aspects of student life in the residential environment, work environment, sports environment, and so on? And how do we know (assess) that these experiences are actually leading to global learning, to a changed perspective on self and the world? On large campuses, these questions cannot be answered by some central administrative office. Campus tradition and campus politics require that these questions be answered at the level of dean (or even department chair). On smaller campuses, these questions will typically be answered by a campuswide committee and discussed by the entire faculty and ultimately articulated by the president.

7

GETTING FROM
HERE TO THERE

Making Internationalization Happen

T here are three main ways that the SIO, as a middle manager change agent, can accelerate the internationalization process, make it more central to the campus mission, and make it more comprehensive across campus. They are presented here progressing from the approach that is within the direct purview of most SIOs to the approach that requires more indirect strategies but has the greatest potential for change.

Building a Pocket of Greatness

The first is to build a "pocket of greatness" (Collins, 2005, pp. 14, 28–31) in the international office. This will likely involve hiring key administrators, perhaps retraining some and imbuing all with a passionate commitment to the office's campus (and perhaps off-campus) mission. In some ways, this is the easiest avenue to broader campus impact because it involves a unit that is largely within the direct control of the SIO. But this is also the most indirect route to campus transformation. It is tempting for SIOs to spend much creative time designing and redesigning their office structure and staffing because it is so close and is most susceptible to their *executive* authority. But the greatest changes always flow from the assertion of *legislative* authority, that is, from persuasion, coalition building, and large-goal-focused persistence. As Peter Drucker famously observed, "Management is doing things right; leadership is doing the right things." Even managing a great office, then, does not make for great things. Nonetheless, surrounding oneself with talented, creative, committed, and effective staff is a precondition to permitting a focus on larger cross-campus issues.

Promoting a Small Program to Campus Prominence

The second way in which the SIO can strengthen internationalization is to help a limited but high-quality and well-led program in an individual unit (department, college, or even administrative office) become a true campus program with high visibility, external funding, and broader participation. This involves working with partners outside the international office to model an approach with proven effectiveness to extend global learning. This is inevitably an incremental process, but breakthroughs can occur with a sudden infusion of outside funding and recognition. The key partner along this path to change is usually campus faculty.

An example of this approach is the unusual linkage between Old Dominion University's (ODU's) physical therapy department and the Universidad Católica Santo Domingo (Dominican Republic). Moving through doors opened by Physicians for Peace (headquartered near ODU's main campus in Norfolk, Virginia), the international office supported the Health Sciences College's innovation for graduate student teaching and learning in the capital of the Dominican Republic. In 2005 the lead faculty member in this project received the Provost Award for Leadership in International Education. Subsequently, ODU established the Center for Global Health in 2012 to coordinate programs with community organizations in several world regions. Over the long term the outreach effort has been truly a win-win-win situation for campus, community, and international partners. The Cherrington Global Scholars program supporting study abroad scholarships at the University of Denver has likewise had a profound impact on the identity of the institution (Nolan & Hunter, 2012, pp. 139–140).

Leveraging the Process of Campus Transformation

The third way that the SIO can accelerate campus internationalization is to leverage a larger aspect of institutional transformation for the purpose of broader internationalization. This approach involves senior campus leadership and has the greatest long-term potential for comprehensive internationalization. The broadest change agendas at a college or university will usually be determined by the president or—for academic matters—delegated to the chief academic officer. The inputs for this change agenda may well include the SIO and other stakeholders who support broader internationalization. But even when the main lines of change are not directly international, the SIO can leverage them for broader internationalization. For example, when a president commits to making an urban (ODU, Norfolk, Virginia), rural (Murray State University, Murray, Kentucky), or commuter (Portland State University) campus more residential, this opens the way for more effective internationalization, especially in terms of campus programming and international study. The key partners in this process are usually senior administrators.

Being a change agent in international education means more than having certain leadership and management skills, including the ability to mobilize campus resources toward strategic goals. Those goals themselves must be based on current knowledge concerning global trends. The SIO must decide—or provide key advice to campus decision-makers—on what strategic opportunities to pursue. Having up-to-date information on a diverse range of global developments is thus a key lever for change in the hands of the SIO.

Finally, part of the special contribution SIOs make to their campus is their unique perspective on long-term trends in global higher education. The SIO is often the only person on campus who has consistent interaction with professional colleagues in all world regions and is familiar with global trends at all levels and fields of study. This knowledge becomes an indispensable tool, for example, in shaping an international student recruitment and admission strategy. This information is therefore relevant to broad constituencies on campus, such as the mathematics department trying to recruit talented graduate students from eastern Europe, an engineering college trying to expand its undergraduate international enrollment, a health sciences faculty trying to expand its Middle Eastern enrollment, or a graduate program director trying to evaluate prospects for an executive or a joint-degree program with a foreign partner. As indicated earlier, this knowledge is also relevant to the undergraduate curriculum on campus, especially the general education curriculum.

8

LESSONS FOR THE SIO

Studies that emphasize the "voluntary" relationship between leader and those the leader is trying to lead are relevant to academic institutions. This is certainly applicable to the role of the SIO within those organizations. The SIO has to work with and through others to get anything done or changed. At best, the SIO has a good deal of "legislative" authority and much less "executive" authority. SIO legitimacy therefore appears to come mainly from networking among key campus stakeholders and longevity in the role. What follows is a discussion of lessons for the SIO, including the role that perception plays in the change process, the role of the middle manager in academic institutions, and how SIOs see the skills needed to be effective.

Perception and Legitimacy

In an increasingly connected and webcast world, the claim that "perception is reality" has taken on new and enhanced meaning. To be sure, reality still counts, but in the context of a college or university, perception is critically important as well. Any academic or student services administrator, including the SIO, depends on many others for his or her support, and that support is basically freely given. Faculty can invest their time in other priorities, administrators can work on other important projects, and students can be drawn into technology or pop culture fads. The SIO can only facilitate change, not mandate it. "True leadership," said Collins (2005), "only exists if people follow when they have the freedom not to" (p. 13). Thus, SIO legitimacy, the perception that SIOs are qualified, experienced, insightful, and respectful, is a crucial element in the ability of SIOs to lead change. In a review of her 25-year career as SIO at the University of Richmond, Uliana Gabara (AIEA president, 2006–2007) repeatedly emphasized the importance of being viewed as a *colleague* among Richmond faculty, the key stakeholder group in the internationalization process (Gabara, 2015; Streitwieser & Ogden, 2016).

In support of their legitimacy, it is clearly an advantage in the United States if SIOs have a record of academic achievement and a natural academic home department in addition to their administrative role in internationalization. Increasingly, senior positions in international education administration in the United States now expect the doctoral (or other terminal) degree (although rarely directly related to internationalization until recently) and some traditional academic experience. But extensive international experience, language skills, and contacts in key funding agencies can all enhance the perception of the SIO's value to potential supporters.

Recent interviews with 8 SIOs who had worked in 10 different countries highlighted the importance of developing a breadth of experience, in either another sector, another higher education institution, or another country. The interviewees also indicated that an increased emphasis on research-informed internationalization means that SIOs should foster their analytical skills, possibly undertaking further study in the field. Whatever learning pathway SIOs undertake, it is important for them to continually update their knowledge and understanding of their own context, both internally, in terms of knowing the institution and its priorities and practices, and externally, in terms of how other institutions and countries are performing, how national priorities for internationalization are evolving, and how global trends are shifting (Lewis, 2016).

Academic and administrative leaders may well bring different strengths to the SIO role. A recent Canadian study noted the advantages of each. Advantages of the academic leader include his or her presumed influence with academic colleagues and ability to forge direct partnerships through research contacts that may generate other international activities. A tenured academic may be less likely to move and thus have a stronger dedication to the institution. The administrative leader, in contrast, may bring experience from other institutions; have influence with leaders elsewhere; have industry connections that can promote international activities; and, if he or she holds a long-term contract, be better positioned to undertake long-term planning (Crane, 2016).

Finally, as observed previously, the perception of the international office directed by the SIO as a well-managed and effective unit is also crucial to the ability of the SIO to lead institutional change. Bolman and Deal (2013) noted that "social interpretations" of reality play a key role in how leaders are perceived and how leaders lead change.

Longevity can play a key role in the SIO's legitimacy and influence on campus. Long tenure usually means that the SIO has experienced the ups and downs of campus funding, transitions in campus leadership, and triumphs in alumni success along with other faculty and staff. Some of the most influential SIOs around the world in recent decades have had very long tenure at a single institution, for example, Jack Van de Water at Oregon State University, John Hudzik at Michigan State University, Axel Markert at the University of Tübingen, Nico Jooste at Nelson Mandela University, and Uliana Gabara at the University of Richmond. These leaders have demonstrated that, in the long run, change over time can add up to truly sustainable internationalization.

But even longevity does not ensure continuity in campus internationalization. As Van de Water (2006) noted, "The arrival of a new president and a new provost . . . should be equated to moving to a new institution. Most all the work done previously to establish credibility with the central administration is 'out the window'" (p. 59). Perhaps a bit of hyperbole, this observation has in fact been confirmed by numerous SIOs who, after years of success advancing an internationalization agenda, have found that agenda—and sometimes their careers—at risk with the arrival of a new president or provost (Heyl & Damron, 2014; Merkx & Nolan, 2015). Maria Krane (2015), SIO at three different institutions (AIEA president, 2003–2004), addressed the inevitable churn of senior leadership philosophically: "Like a modern Proteus, I had to be versatile, adapting to each new situation and staying in the revolving door long enough to advance the international agenda, somehow" (p. 111).

Changes in senior leadership may also lead to negative outcomes for the SIO. This was evident from a survey of 25 SIOs in 16 different countries who identified key challenges they faced. One of the most frequent challenges mentioned was the recognition of the SIO role in the institutional hierarchy. This meant that achievements were not recognized and rewarded or that roles were not properly defined, leading to lack of coordination and tensions. Reporting lines were also often an issue, either because they were not clearly defined or because the SIO reported to a supervisor with little interest in internationalization (Carbonell & Ripoll, 2014). Some may survive these vicissitudes; others may choose to move on. Whatever the choice of the SIO, it is never good for the institution when such tensions persist over time.

Conversely, a new SIO has the advantage of having been selected with high hopes for expanding internationalization and expectations of strong, new leadership. In short, there are often relatively narrow windows in both situations that the SIO must be prepared to exploit. Despite the challenges, many would probably agree that the SIO role is "the hardest job you'll ever love" (Nolan, 2015).

Traits

Dismissing the idea that there is such a thing as a "leadership personality" or leadership qualities, Drucker (2001) asserted that leadership is "mundane, unromantic, and boring. Its essence is performance" (p. 268). This view is confirmed by Collins (2005), whose leader who takes his or her company from "good to great" is a "compelling combination of personal humility and professional will" (p. 11). Collins's "hedgehog concept"—the personality mix of the transformational leader—combines passion for the organization's mission with insight into its unique contribution and understanding of its "resource engine" (pp. 17–19).

Bolman and Deal (2013) rejected most of the oversimplified models of leadership that focus on specific traits, even though there is considerable consensus on a few, such as vision, communication skills, and ability to inspire trust. They concluded, "Wise leaders understand their own strengths, work to expand them, and build diverse teams that can offer an organization leadership in all four modes—structural, political, human resource, and symbolic" (p. 369). Likewise, the ACE authors (ACE, 2001) concluded that "there is no prototype of the successful leader" but that all successful change leaders in their studies were "principle-driven," persistent, focused on moving the change process forward, and not distracted by unexpected obstacles or unanticipated conflicts (pp. 14–16).

Process

This component of leadership includes two kinds of processes. One focuses on the interaction between leaders and followers. The other focuses on the process that leaders use to analyze relevant variables to their leadership and the change situation. The change process is inherently interactive. This means that change leaders must pay attention to process. Especially in academic settings, process is crucial because of the diffuse nature of power in the institution.

As middle managers, SIOs are usually involved in two change processes at once: leading a process of development and change within the international unit(s) they direct, and trying to lead the institution as a whole to greater internationalization. Internally, this means that SIOs need to pay attention to their staff and the imperative to hire the right people ("getting the right people on the bus"; Collins, 2005, pp. 13–17) and to developing, mentoring, and motivating others to a shared vision and high performance. Even in settings where SIOs do not have authority to hire their staff, SIOs can play an important role in their professional development. Beyond the office, SIOs enter a world of constant coalition building, communicating, informing, and rewarding. Bolman and Deal (2013) found that both effective and successful leaders found a way to balance internal (mainly human resource) responsibilities with external (mainly networking) responsibilities. Likewise, the ACE authors (2001) concluded that successful change leaders know instinctively (or from hard-won experience) that "change initiatives are as likely to be derailed over disagreements about process as they are about substance" (p. 18).

Resisters

Much of the change literature includes a discussion of the role that resisters to change play in the change process. Senge (2006) in *The Fifth Discipline: The Art and Practice of the Learning Organization* said that most strategic planning tends to be reactive and short term and does not pay sufficient attention to the "balancing processes" beneath the surface of an organization that obstruct change toward the planning goals. This is relevant to both the corporate and nonprofit sectors because there are so many forms that resistance to change can take. In the campus setting, resistance is further complicated by the inherited shared governance model. In this setting, resistance to change can be cloaked in principled stances, such as "It [the proposed change] doesn't meet standards of faculty or administration consultation" or "It violates who we are as an institution." One corporate executive, who left a university dean's position in frustration, learned belatedly that the tenured faculty could, if they wished, be "a thousand points of no" (Collins, 2005, p. 14). One university plan for comprehensive internationalization, for example, specifically made mention of the importance of overcoming "faculty resistance" (Lacy, 2006 p. 42).

Resisters to change are found in any organization. It is human nature. Many inevitably perceive change as unsettling or even threatening. But resistance can be neutralized with a few well-recognized techniques. First, build an open, inclusive process in which the proposed change is discussed. Resisters deserve a forum to express their views, which may also be an opportunity to win them over. Nolan (2015), an SIO at 4 universities over more than 20 years, noted that "interactive, highly participatory approaches to planning and implementation work best in almost all circumstances" (p. 181). Second, enlist the help of resisters in shaping the final version of the proposed change. Leaders understand the truth of the following adage: "People support what they help create." Third, do not include naysayers in the senior leadership team responsible for implementing the change. Fourth, broadly and loudly communicate early successes in the change process to neutralize residual negative views.

Resistance to internationalization also takes many forms. The echoes will be familiar to any SIO: "Our universities are the best in the world—just look at the global rankings. Why should students study anywhere else?" "The language limitations of international students place too many demands on our faculty." "How can we be sure that our partner programs are of the same quality as on-campus courses?" "Isn't summer faculty travel abroad just a form of academic tourism?" SIOs must have ready responses to such resistance based on the real experiences and testimonials of their students and faculty.

The SIO can play a role in all of these strategies by providing key information to senior leadership and the campus at large, by promoting examples of progress, and by providing settings (e.g., advisory groups) where all views will be heard and conflicts can be resolved before they become campus confrontations. In the end, complacency, a skeptical faculty, and apathetic students—not active opposition—are often the more common obstacles to the change agenda.

When the SIO is developing an inclusive campus conversation, it is critically important to involve administrative staff, including those who, in some national contexts, have often been left behind in the internationalization process. Feeling excluded and uninformed provides excellent reason for resistance. As institutions embrace a more comprehensive approach, they will find that the scope, volume, and complexity of international activities increase, and it is wise to see administrative staff not only as essential but also as equal partners in the process (Hunter, 2018).

The Role of the Middle Manager

As noted previously, surveys in the United States have repeatedly confirmed that SIOs are almost always middle managers, not necessarily a member of the senior leadership team but at least reporting to a member of that team (AIEA, 2015). The role of the middle manager can be frustrating, but it can also be rewarding. For one thing, there is often a good deal of autonomy in such a role, especially on the college or university campus. The prime example of this is the department chair. Although chairs report to deans, they have considerable autonomy to make decisions regarding the curriculum and the hiring, salary, and tenure of faculty, with only occasional interventions by the dean or senior academic officer. If change is derailed for some reason, the tenured chair can always retreat to a regular faculty position. Not surprisingly, the department chair has a reputation for balkanization—for encouraging centrifugal forces that protect the silo interest of the academic unit.

Most SIOs, like department chairs, have a fairly well-defined portfolio and are expected to raise performance of the units that report to them (e.g., expanding study abroad, building international enrollment, and enhancing international student and scholar services and support) and engage the campus globally in whatever ways are most feasible. Moreover, the middle manager on a college campus typically encounters a wider range of campus constituencies than does much of senior leadership. For example, SIOs develop contacts globally that create a unique network across many academic disciplines and other campus stakeholders. Finally, for the middle manager there is a certain freedom that comes with professional mobility. If senior leadership remains cautious and change averse over a prolonged period (which is unlikely), the middle manager can wait or leave (Heyl & Damron, 2014; Kotter, 1996). If middle managers are tenured faculty members, they can return to their academic department and pursue change there.

The middle manager, then, has a range of influence. This is not executive authority, the kind that vests with the CEO or other senior academic leaders. But the middle manager always has the power of language and innovation, the power of inclusion, and the power of cross-divisional alliances. That middle managers can make big change happen was illustrated by Kotter and Cohen (2002) with a company that changed its entire purchasing system (a big deal) when a middle manager (with help from a summer intern) demonstrated that the company was purchasing 424 different kinds of gloves for its different factories. The manager put all the different kinds of gloves on the board room table (with widely varying price tags) and invited all the division chiefs and vice presidents in to view the gloves. Very soon, the company radically changed its purchasing system to achieve significant cost savings (Kotter & Cohen, 2002). The SIO can sometimes have a similar impact by revealing the ineffectiveness of uncoordinated efforts and missed opportunities internationally (Lacy, 2004, 2015).

As a middle manager the SIO is continuously involved in looking in several directions at once. "They must enroll the hearts and minds of many employees in creating solutions. They must also enroll top management in this vision to create the mandate they do not initially possess" (Watkins & Marsick, 1993, p. 205). This means they are constantly developing the campus network between faculty and other administrative units that work against silos and toward integration and comprehensiveness. This is certainly a challenging position, and it is not for the faint of heart, but its rewards are great as well. As middle manager, the SIO can develop into a *leader-manager* who can both inspire change and help manage, direct, and sustain it (Krane, 2015).

Let us now look at how SIOs see themselves and the qualities, knowledge, and skills they need to be effective.

SIOs on Leadership

Over the past several years, a modest research agenda has emerged that focuses on what SIOs think of leadership, key leadership skills, and the context in which they work. In 1999, Tom Hoemecke, then SIO at the University of North Texas, led a research team in AIEA that produced the first survey of SIOs on these topics. AIEA has reported on subsequent surveys in 2006, 2012, 2015, and 2018 (see www.aieaworld.org for these surveys). The AIEA surveys aim to develop a collective biography of SIOs at U.S. universities and to identify the qualities, knowledge, and skills that SIOs think are important for their success.

In 2007, a task force within NAFSA's International Education Leadership Knowledge Community (IEL) undertook to extend the AIEA research to "generate a snapshot of where the international education leadership is right now, from the perspective of SIOs themselves" (Lambert, Nolan, Peterson, & Pierce, 2007, p. 2). The task force surveyed 35 senior (in both position and experience) international education officers in 2 rounds of surveys on personal qualities (traits), background knowledge, specialized knowledge, functional skills, and specialized skills.

In 2016, EAIE dedicated an issue of its membership magazine, *Forum*, to "The New International Officer." Editor Laura Rumbley posed the question of the future role of the SIO in terms of how to effectively manage internationalization and move the institution forward, thus clearly connecting internationalization to a process of institutional change. Attempts to answer the question were addressed by a range of different actors involved in internationalization, not only in Europe but also in Canada and Australia. In particular, the question was asked to participants at EAIE's 2016 annual conference to find out what SIOs do and how they see their role.

Taken together these surveys present a collective portrait of the SIO that confirms much of the research on leadership but also emphasizes the centrality of the middle manager role that most SIOs fill. That is, under personal qualities, the SIOs surveyed by the NAFSA task force cited "diplomacy and tact" and "imagination and energy" as mentioned most frequently, and "teamwork/flexibility/listening" and "administrative experience/knowing one's home institution" ranked at the top in terms of importance. AIEA's surveys have consistently found that interpersonal communication, visioning, and intercultural competence were the most highly valued skills in their work. The EAIE focus groups raised the issue, perhaps inherent to the position, of whether the role was more strategic or operational, pointing out that while these administrators aspired to be more strategic, often day-to-day management took up the bulk of their time. While they were all involved in one way or another in strategic planning efforts, they were not all satisfied with the degree of involvement (Weimar, 2016).

Although not conclusive, these results suggest, among other things, that the SIO role demands skills in such practical matters as strategic planning and in the more amorphous skills of leadership and communication. As supportive of the latter, SIOs ranked energy and passion, overseas experience, and cross-cultural skills as highly valued traits and skills. Ethics fell slightly below these top priorities but only slightly so. In recent years, many SIOs have increasingly added knowledge of business principles and practices and entrepreneurial skills as talents required to fulfill the revenue-generation expectations of the position (AIEA, 2015; Deschamps & Lee, 2015).

Although not recognized explicitly in these surveys, there is an emerging interest in the SIO as scholar-practitioner (or practitioner-researcher), that is, as a professional able to contribute to the understanding and improvement of practice through (typically) social-science-based research. Not all SIOs are expected to pursue active research agendas, but those who do will help shape the field of international higher education as an academic discipline. Their efforts, increasingly recognized at the institutional and professional levels, will help colleagues pursue evidence-based practice (Deardorff & van Gaalen, 2012; Hunter & Rumbley, 2016). For some, research in international education not only informs professional practice but also guides career development. As Krane (2015) noted, "My research served as my sense of direction as I . . . adapted to new and challenging situations. It was truly my compass" (p. 126).

SIOs may thus see themselves as requiring a knowledge and skill set that is unique to their position—with an emphasis on face-to-face communication and advocacy skills, knowledge of one's own institution and wider higher education trends, and a broad background in international affairs and cultures. How do they put these qualities to work in concrete settings? How does the SIO lead change? Many SIOs, along with most of their middle manager colleagues, toil in a more or less persistent condition of benign neglect, with supportive rhetoric from senior administrators but little perceptible advance of the international agenda on campus. Others, however, achieve breakthroughs that put their institutions on the road to comprehensive internationalization. It is hoped the discussion in these pages helps illuminate the difference between these two scenarios.

9

CONCLUDING REMARKS

SIO alert: There is a countercurrent relevant to SIO work in the United States and around the world. This current is driven by a range of discontents—with the impact of globalization on local and regional economies, with fears of global terrorism, and with anxieties over south–north migration. Populist and authoritarian leaders have exploited these discontents by (re)shaping democratic politics and mobilizing national, ethnic, and regional grievances. These forces have produced a set of developments unique since the end of the Cold War.

In their eagerness to embrace the momentum of international education at the beginning of the twenty-first century, many SIOs were ready to dismiss Amy Chua's (2002) important book *World on Fire*, which argued that the "new world order" was bound to be a dangerous and disrupted place (Heyl, 2017; Woolf, 2002).

Indeed, it may well be that international education leaders will view the past 20 to 25 years in their field as a kind of "golden age" when many factors—the end of the Cold War, the end of apartheid in South Africa, expanded government support for new global partnerships and increasing student mobility, the arrival of the "first globals" generation on campus, the dawn of the Internet, and the advance of a global economy—all combined to raise the visibility, prestige, and resources of international education (Loveland, 2010). Today's era is much changed from those heady days, but it continues to call for committed SIO leadership (Fischer, 2017).

In this newly challenging environment, SIOs may want to consider a number of responses. First, SIOs must remember that international education is first and foremost about *education* (de Wit, 2015). This means that SIOs should work with colleagues, in particular with curricular leaders in academic departments, to see that these issues—and responses to them—are part of a globalized curriculum. Second, SIOs should learn more about these grievances, in particular, as they manifest themselves in their communities, states, provinces, and regions. Third, SIOs should be advocates for international populations (faculty, students, staff, local immigrant groups, and visitors) whenever they are targets of these grievances, however misplaced those grievances may be (Rhoades, 2017). Finally, SIOs should employ their unique networks to develop public statements that enrich dialogue on these topics.

These suggested responses are in no way intended to diminish the importance of continuing to lead innovation in global learning and partnerships, across the institution and internationally. But they do indicate that SIOs must now increasingly link their traditional agenda to the domestic and local issues and concerns of their stakeholders. In this way, the SIO role will indeed have come full circle (Bogenschild & Latz, 2018).

This is a big agenda, much bigger than the day-to-day whirl of work in international offices at colleges and universities around the world. But international educators are well prepared and well situated to take on this big agenda and to encourage their colleagues, students, and institutions to be truly active global citizens. A maximally effective SIO would share in such a vision—for his or her university, for its community setting, for higher education, for global education, for the future.

REFERENCES

Altbach, P. G. (2016). *Global perspectives on higher education.* Baltimore, MD: Johns Hopkins University Press.

Altbach, P. G., & de Wit, H. (2017, Spring). Trump and the coming revolution in higher education internationalization. *International Higher Education, 89,* 3–5.

Altbach, P. G., & de Wit, H. (2018, February 23). The challenge to higher education internationalisation. *University World News,* No. 494.

Altbach, P. G., Mihut, G., & Salmi, J. (2016, July 1). Are international advisory councils the future? *University World News* (Global Education), No. 420.

American Council on Education. (1999). *On change III: Taking charge of change; A primer for colleges and universities.* Washington, DC: Author.

American Council on Education. (2001). *On change V: Riding the waves of change; Insights from transforming institutions.* Washington, DC: Author.

American Council on Education. (2005). *Internationalization in U.S. higher education: The student perspective.* Washington, DC: Author.

American Council on Education. (2013). *Internationalization in action: The internationalization committee; Strategies for success.* Retrieved July 10, 2018, from http://www.acenet.edu/newsroom/Pages/Intlz-in-Action-2013-January.aspx

American Council on Education. (2017a). *CIGE model for comprehensive internationalization.* Retrieved from http://www.acenet.edu/newsroom/Pages/CIGEModel-for-Comprehensive-internationalization.aspx

American Council on Education. (2017b). *Mapping internationalization on U.S. campuses: 2017 edition.* Retrieved from http://www.acennet.edu/newsroom/Documents/Mapping-internationalization-2017.pdf

Association of International Education Administrators. (2015). *A [2014] survey on senior international education officers, their institutions and offices.* Retrieved from http://www.aieaworld.org/assets/docs/Surveys/sio%20survey%20summary.pdf

Association of International Education Administrators. (2017a). *The SIO profile: A preliminary analysis of the survey on senior international education officers, their institutions and offices* (2017). Retrieved from https://www.aieaworld.org/assets/docs/Surveys/final-2017%20executive%20summary_sio%20profile%20survey.pdf

Association of International Education Administrators. (2017b). *They were at the beginning: Lessons from leaders in internationalization [Interview with Riall Nolan]*. Retrieved from http://www.aieaworld.org/lessons-from-leaders-in-izn#nolan

Beelen, J., & Jones, E. (2015, Winter). Looking back at 15 years of internationalisation at home. *Forum*, 6–8.

Bogenschild, T. & Latz, G. (2018). Connecting with the Community. In D. K. Deardorff & H. Charles (Eds.), *Leading internationalization: A handbook for international education leaders* (pp. 114–119). Sterling, VA: Stylus.

Bolman, L. G., & Deal, T. E. (2013). *Reframing organizations: Artistry, choice, and leadership* (5th ed.). San Francisco, CA: Jossey-Bass.

Brewer, E., Charles, H., & Ferguson, A. (2015, February). *Strategic planning for internationalization in higher education*. Durham, NC: AIEA. Retrieved from http://aiea.memberclicks.net/assets/docs/Occasional Papers/occasional%20paper-%20strategic%20planning%20in%20 a%20university%20context%202015.pdf

Brewer, E., & Cunningham, K. (Eds.). (2009). *Integrating study abroad into the curriculum: Theory and practice across the disciplines*. Sterling, VA: Stylus.

Brewer, E., & Leask, B. (2012). The internationalization of the curriculum. In D. K. Deardorff, H. de Wit, J. Heyl, & T. Adams (Eds.), *The SAGE handbook of international higher education* (pp. 245–265). Thousand Oaks, CA: SAGE.

Cameron, K. S., & Quinn, R. E. (2011). *Diagnosing and changing organizational culture* (3rd ed.). San Francisco, CA: Jossey-Bass.

Carbonell, J. A., & Ripoll, L. (2014, July 4). Who killed the international officer [EAIE blog]? Retrieved from https://www.eaie.org/blog/who-killed-the-international-officer.html

Charles, H. & Pynes, P. (2018). The senior international officer as entrepreneur. In D. K. Deardorff & H. Charles (Eds.), *Leading internationalization: A handbook for international education leaders* (pp. 129–134). Sterling, VA: Stylus.

Chua, A. (2002). *World on fire: How exporting free market democracy breeds ethnic hatred and global instability*. New York, NY: Doubleday.

Collins, J. (2001). *Good to great: Why some companies make the leap . . . and others don't*. New York, NY: HarperCollins.

Collins, J. (2005). *Good to great and the social sectors: Why business thinking is not the answer*. New York, NY: HarperCollins.

Crane, L. (2016, Winter). Leadership styles in the international office. *Forum*, 23–25.

Deardorff, D. K. (2018). Outcomes assessment for senior international officers. In D. K. Deardorff & H. Charles (Eds.), *Leading internationalization: A handbook for international education leaders* (pp. 73–80). Sterling, VA: Stylus.

Deardorff, D. K., & Charles, H. (Eds.). (2018). *Leading internationalization: A handbook for international education leaders.* Sterling, VA: Stylus.

Deardorff, D. K., de Wit, H., Heyl, J., & Adams, T. (Eds.). (2012). *The SAGE handbook of international higher education.* Thousand Oaks, CA: SAGE.

Deardorff, D. K., & van Gaalen, A. (2012). Outcomes assessment in the internationalization of higher education. In D. K. Deardorff, H. de Wit, J. Heyl, & T. Adams (Eds.), *The SAGE handbook of international higher education* (pp. 167–189). Thousand Oaks, CA: SAGE.

Deardorff, D. K., Rosenbaum, K. L. & Teekens, H. (2018). Ethics in leading internationalization. In D. K. Deardorff & H. Charles (Eds.), *Leading internationalization: A handbook for international education leaders* (pp. 150–156). Sterling, VA: Stylus.

Deschamps, E., & Lee, J. J. (2015). Internationalization as mergers and acquisitions: Senior international officers' entrepreneurial strategies and activities in public universities. *Journal of Studies in International Education, 19*(2), 122–139.

de Wit, H. (2015, Spring). Is the international university the future for higher education? *International Higher Education, 80,* 7.

de Wit, H., & Altbach, P. G. (in press). Higher education as a global reality. In J. C. Shin & P. N. Teixeira (Eds.), *Encyclopedia of international higher education systems and institutions.* Dordrecht, the Netherlands: Springer.

de Wit, H., Hunter, F., Howard, L., & Egron-Polak, E. (2015). *Internationalisation of higher education.* Brussels, Belgium: European Parliament, Directorate-General for Internal Policies.

Drucker, P. F. (2001). *The essential Drucker.* New York, NY: HarperBusiness.

Fielden, J. (2012). *The management of internationalisation in universities: Internationalisation of European higher education* [EUA/ACA Handbook]. Berlin, Germany: Dr. Josef Raabe Verlag.

Fischer, K. (2017, May 31). International educators confront a new political reality—and find a new resolve. *The Chronicle of Higher Education.* Retrieved from http://www.chronicle.com/article/International-Educators/240220

Friedman, T. L. (1999). *The lexus and the olive tree: Understanding globalization.* New York, NY: Farrar, Straus and Giroux.

Gabara, U. (2015). Nine pretty hard lessons from twenty-five years as a senior international officer. In G. W. Merkx & R. W. Nolan (Eds.), *Internationalizing the academy: Lessons of leadership in higher education* (pp. 127–149). Cambridge, MA: Harvard Education Press.

Gates, R. M. (2016). *A passion for leadership: Lessons on change and reform from fifty years of public service.* New York, NY: Knopf.

Green, M. F., & Olson, C. (2003). *Internationalizing the campus: A user's guide.* Washington, DC: American Council on Education.

Green, M. F., & Schoenberg, R. (2006). *Where faculty live: Internationalizing the disciplines.* Washington, DC: American Council on Education.

Grinkevich, Y., & Shabanova, M. (2016, Winter). New times, new challenges. *Forum*, 6–7.

Heyl, J. D. (2007). *The senior international officer (SIO) as change agent.* Durham, NC: Association of International Education Administrators.

Heyl, J. D. (2017, October 26). *International higher education in the age of Trump.* IELeaders.net. Retrieved from http://www.ieleaders.net/

Heyl, J. D., & Damron, D. (2014). Should I stay or should I go? Career dilemmas for international educators. *International Educator, 23*(5), 50–53.

Hunter, F. (2018, Winter). Training administrative staff to become key players in the internationalization of higher education. *International Higher Education, 92,* 16–17.

Hunter, F., de Wit, H., & Howard, L. (2016). Key trends in internationalisation of higher education: Are we heading in the right direction? In M. Stiasny & T. Gore (Eds.), *Going global, connecting cultures, forging futures* (pp. 4–12). London, UK: Institute of Education Press.

Hunter, F., & Rumbley, L. (2016). Exploring a possible future for the scholar-practitioner. In B. Streitwieser & A. C. Ogden (Eds.), *International higher education's scholar-practitioners: Bridging research and practice* (pp. 297–308). Oxford, UK: Symposium Books.

Hunter, F., & Sparnon, N. (2018). Warp and weft: Weaving internationalization into institutional life. In D. Proctor & L. Rumbley (Eds.), *The future agenda for internationalization in higher education: Next generation insights into research, policy and practice* (pp. 155–167). Abingdon, UK: Routledge.

Institute of International Education. (2018). *Open Doors 2017.* Retrieved from https://www.iie.org/Research-and-Insights/Open-Doors/Fact-Sheets -and-Infographics/Infographics

Knight, J. (2015). International universities: Misunderstandings and emerging models? *Journal of Studies in International Education, 9*(2), 107–121.

Kotter, J. P. (1996). *Leading change.* Boston, MA: Harvard Business School Press.

Kotter, J. P., & Cohen, D. S. (2002). *The heart of change: Real-life stories of how people change their organizations.* Boston, MA: Harvard Business School Press.

Krane, M. C. S. (2015). The senior international officer: A modern Proteus? In G. W. Merkx & R. W. Nolan (Eds.), *Internationalizing the academy: Lessons of leadership in higher education* (pp. 111–126). Cambridge, MA: Harvard Education Press.

Lacy, W. (2004, Fall). The seven habits of highly effective universities: Enhancing international learning, discovery and engagement. *IIE Networker*, 40–42.

Lacy, W. (2006, Spring). Internationalizing the campus through institutional leadership. *IIE Networker*, 41–42.

Lacy, W. (2015). A contemporary odyssey to senior international leadership. In G. W. Merkx & R. W. Nolan (Eds.), *Internationalizing the academy: Lessons of leadership in higher education* (pp. 183–198). Cambridge, MA: Harvard Education Press.

Lambert, S., Nolan, R., Peterson, N., & Pierce, D. (2007). *Critical skills and knowledge for senior campus international leaders.* Retrieved from http://www.nafsa.org/_/Document/_/delphi.pdf

Leask, B. & Charles, H. (2018). Internationalizing the curriculum. In D. K. Deardorff & H. Charles (Eds.), *Leading internationalization: A handbook for international education leaders* (pp. 65–72). Sterling, VA: Stylus

Leask, B., Green, W., & Whitsed, C. (2015, Winter). Australia: Internationalization of the curriculum at home. *Forum,* 34–35.

Lewis, V. (2016, Winter). A journey through time and space. *Forum,* 36–38.

Lombardi, J. (1991). American international: Colleges, universities and global education. *International Education Forum, 11*(1), 1–8.

Longoni, D. (2015, Winter). Bold decisions and big results in Italy. *Forum,* 28–30.

Loveland, E. (2006). Education abroad required: An interview with Goucher College president Sanford Ungar. *International Educator, 15*(1), 22–25.

Loveland, E. (2010). The first globals generation. *International Educator, 19*(3), 22–26.

Maringe, F., & Foskett, N. (Eds.). (2010). *Globalization and internationalization in higher education: Theoretical, strategic and management perspectives.* New York, NY: Continuum International.

Marrin, J. (2012). *Leadership for dummies.* San Francisco, CA: John Wiley.

McCarthy, J. S. (2007, June 29). A roadmap for creating the global campus. *The Chronicle of Higher Education,* B12.

McPherson, P. (1994, February 24). A framework for a practice vision: The 1994 state of the university address. *MSU News Bulletin,* p. 6.

Merkx, G. W. (2015). Atlas, Sisyphus, or Odysseus? In G. W. Merkx & R. W. Nolan (Eds.), *Internationalizing the academy: Lessons of leadership in higher education* (pp. 65–85). Cambridge, MA: Harvard Education Press.

Merkx, G. W., & Nolan, R. W. (Eds.). (2015). *Internationalizing the academy: Lessons of leadership in higher education.* Cambridge, MA: Harvard Education Press.

Merkx, G. W., & Nolan, R. W. (2018). Forming alliances and working with administration. In D. K. Deardorff & H. Charles (Eds.), *Leading internationalization: A handbook for international education leaders* (pp. 47–54). Sterling, VA: Stylus.

Mestenhauser, J. A., & Ellingboe, B. J. (2005, November–December). Leadership knowledge and international education. *International Educator, 14,* 37–43.

Murray, D., Goedegebuure, L., van Liempd, H. G., & Vermeulen, M. (2014). *Leadership needs in international higher education in Australia and Europe: Final report of a Delphi study*. Amsterdam, the Netherlands: EAIE/IEAA.

Nolan, R. W. (2015). SIO: The hardest job you'll ever love. In G. W. Merkx & R. W. Nolan (Eds.), *Internationalizing the academy: Lessons of leadership in higher education* (pp. 169–182). Cambridge, MA: Harvard Education Press.

Nolan, R. W. (2018). Strategic planning for senior international officers. In D. K. Deardorff & H. Charles (Eds.), *Leading internationalization: A handbook for international education leaders* (pp. 31–38). Sterling, VA: Stylus.

Nolan, R., & Hunter, F. (2012). Institutional strategies and international programs: Learning from experiences of change. In D. Deardorff, H. de Wit, J. Heyl, & T. Adams (Eds.), *The SAGE handbook of international higher education* (pp. 131–145). Thousand Oaks, CA: SAGE.

Olson, C. L., Green, M. F., & Hill, B. A. (2005). *Building a strategic framework for comprehensive internationalization*. Washington, DC: American Council on Education.

Owen, J. (2011). *How to lead* (3rd ed.). Upper Saddle River, NJ: FT Press.

Paullin, E. (2016, Winter). Breaking down walls: The silo effect. *Forum*, 10–11.

Proctor, D. (2016, Winter). Building bridges. *Forum*, 18–19.

Rhoades, G. (2017, Spring). Backlash against "others." *International Higher Education, 89*, 2–3.

Rumbley, L. (2016, Winter). The new international officer. *Forum, 4*.

Scarboro, D. (2016). The benefits and limits of scholarship and self-expression among international education professionals. In B. Streitwieser & A. C. Ogden (Eds.), *International higher education's scholar-practitioners: Bridging research and practice* (pp. 93–101). Oxford, UK: Symposium Books.

Schein, E. H. (2010). *Organizational culture and leadership* (4th ed.). Hoboken, NJ: John Wiley/Jossey-Bass.

Schlör, W., & Barnes, T. (2012). The strategic management challenge for research I universities. *International Briefs for Higher Education Leaders*, No. 2, 11–13. Retrieved from http://www.acenet.edu/news-room/Documents/International-Briefs-2012-November-Global-Engagement.pdf

Senge, P. M. (2006). *The fifth discipline: The art and practice of the learning organization*. New York, NY: Currency Doubleday.

Siaya, L., Porcelli, M., & Green, M. F. (2002). *One year later: Attitudes about international education since September 11*. Washington, DC: American Council on Education.

Streitwieser, B., & Ogden, A. C. (2016). *International higher education's scholar-practitioners: Bridging research and practice.* Oxford, UK: Symposium Books.

Taylor, J. (2012). Structuring internationalisation: The role of the international office. In RAABE & RAABE (Eds.), *Handbook on internationalisation in higher education* (pp. 1–25). Berlin, Germany: RAABE.

The Chronicle of Higher Education. (2014). *The innovative university: What college presidents think about change in American higher education.* Washington, DC: Author.

University of Missouri–Columbia. (2018). *MU Global Scholars Program.* Retrieved from https://international.missouri.edu/get-involved/faculty-development/global-scholars-program.php

University of the Pacific. (2018). *Pacific 2020R.* Retrieved from http://www.pacific.edu/Documents/marketing/Pacific-2020R-Web.pdf

Vandenberg, L., Thullen, M., & Fear, F. (1986). *A review of literature on leadership with applications on CFS community leadership development programs.* East Lansing, MI: Michigan State University.

Van de Water, J. (2000). The international office: Taking a closer look. *International Educator, 9*(2), 30–33, 37.

Van de Water, J. (2006). Lessons learned: Musings on a 30-year career in international education. *International Educator, 15*(1), 57–61.

Van de Water, J. (2015). International education leadership: Reflections on experience. In G. W. Merkx & R. W. Nolan (Eds.), *Internationalizing the academy: Lessons of leadership in higher education* (pp. 37–52). Cambridge, MA: Harvard Education Press.

van Liempd, H. G. (2013, March 5). *A new style of leadership for internationalization.* European Association for International Education Blog. Retrieved from https://www.eaie.org/blog/leadership-skills-international-education/

Vara, V. (2007, April 16). After GE. *Wall Street Journal*, p. R3.

Watkins, K. E., & Marsick, V. J. (1993). *Sculpting the learning organization: Lessons in the art and science of systemic change.* San Francisco, CA: Jossey-Bass.

Weick, K. E. (1976). Educational organizations as loosely coupled systems. *Administrative Science Quarterly, 21*(1), 1–19.

Weimar, L. (2016, Winter). Who is Europe's senior international officer? *Forum*, 39–41.

Woolf, M. (2002). Harmony and dissonance in international education: The limits of globalisation. *Journal of Studies in International Education, 6*(1), 5–15.

Yukl, G. A. (2005). *Leadership in organizations* (6th ed.). Englewood Cliffs, NJ: Prentice Hall.

ABOUT THE AUTHORS

John D. Heyl is founder and editor of IELeaders.net, a website focusing on senior international officer (SIO) leadership issues. He was professor of history at Illinois Wesleyan University (Bloomington, Illinois) and SIO at the University of Missouri–Columbia and Old Dominion University (Norfolk, Virginia). Heyl is former president (2000–2001) of the Association of International Education Administrators (AIEA), author of *The Senior International Officer (SIO) as Change Agent* (AIEA, 2007), and coeditor of *The SAGE Handbook of International Higher Education* (SAGE, 2012). He holds a BA from Stanford University and a PhD in European history from Washington University–St. Louis.

Fiona J. H. Hunter is based in Italy, where she works as associate director at the Centre for Higher Education Internationalisation (CHEI) at the *Università Cattolica del Sacro Cuore* in Milan. She is coeditor of the *Journal of Studies for International Education* (JSIE) and past president of the European Association for International Education (EAIE). Alongside her role as a researcher, she also works as a consultant and trainer supporting higher education institutions around the world in their internationalization and strategic planning efforts. She holds a doctor of business administration from the University of Bath in the United Kingdom.

Also available from Stylus

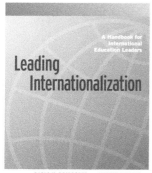

Leading Internationalization

A Handbook for International Education Leaders

Edited by Darla K. Deardorff and Harvey Charles

Foreword by E. Gordon Gee

Afterword by Allan Goodman

"A practical guide for university leadership based on standards of professional practice and the distilled wisdom of highly successful senior international officers, this book shares successful strategies and tactics to advance the global priorities of any campus. It is an essential guide for institutions at every level of internationalization." — ***Brian Whalen, President and CEO, The Forum on Education Abroad***

This volume provides senior professionals in international education, increasingly known as senior international officers (SIOs), with the foundational knowledge that informs leadership practices, together with suggested strategies for implementing and developing the wide range of functions, activities, and skills associated with comprehensive internationalization that will ensure effective support for their institutions' educational missions in today's globalized and interdependent world.

This book addresses strategic leadership issues in internationalization including strategic planning, shaping the curriculum, recruiting students, risk management, and developing partnerships. Throughout, the Association of International Education Administrators' (AIEA) Standards of Professional Practice for SIOs and International Education Leaders (reproduced in the appendix) are integrated as a point of reference, providing a much-needed guide for international education leaders.

22883 Quicksilver Drive
Sterling, VA 20166-2019   Subscribe to our e-mail alerts: www.Styluspub.com

The Association of International Education Administrators (AIEA) is the only association dedicated exclusively to senior leaders in international higher education.

AIEA brings international education leaders into dialogue with each other, their counterparts around the world, organizations that promote international education, and organizations concerned with the shaping and management of international higher education. AIEA gives members opportunities to join forces, share institutional strategies, and provide an effective voice on matters of public policy.

The purposes of AIEA are the following:

- Provide an effective voice on significant issues within international education at all levels
- Improve and promote international education leadership and internationalization within institutions of higher education
- Establish and maintain a professional network among international education institutional leaders
- Cooperate in appropriate ways with other national and international groups having similar interests.

AIEA provides resources and professional development opportunities through an annual international conference, a weeklong leadership academy, thematic forums, a Presidential Fellows program, and other mentorship programs. In addition to copublishing *Leading Internationalization: A Handbook for International Education Leaders*, AIEA also copublished *The Sage Handbook of International Higher Education* edited by Darla K. Deardorff, Hans de Wit, John D. Heyl, and Tony Adams.

AIEA was founded in 1982. The Secretariat is headquartered in Durham, North Carolina, the United States, and the association comprises over 1000 members from over 35 countries.

www.aieaworld.org